W9-BRZ-124

CHRIST'S CALL TO DISCIPLESHIP

CHRIST'S CALL TO DISCIPLESHIP

JAMES MONTGOMERY BOICE

MOODY PRESS

CHICAGO

© 1986 by
THE MOODY BIBLE INSTITUTE
OF CHICAGO

Library of Congress Cataloging-in-Publication Data

Boice, James Montgomery, 1938-
    Christ's call to discipleship.

    1. Christian life — Presbyterian authors.   I. Title.
BV4501.2.B614   1986   248.4'851   85-28460
ISBN 0-8024-1397-8

1 2 3 4 5 6 7 Printing/RR/Year 87 86
Printed in the United States of America

To Him
who denied Himself
and took up His cross
for us

Contents

CHAPTER   PAGE

Preface   9
The Meaning of Discipleship
1. The Call to Discipleship   13
2. In the School of Christ   25
3. Taking Up the Cross   35
The Path of Discipleship
4. The Path of Obedience   47
5. The Path of Service   59
6. The Path of Humility   71
7. Traveling Light   81
8. "But Is He with Us?"   93
The Cost of Discipleship
9. Counting the Cost   105
10. New Relationships   115
11. No Turning Back   125
The Rewards of Discipleship
12. The Happy Christian   137
13. Present Blessings, Plus Persecutions   149
14. Christ with Us Always   159

Preface

"Why do you call me, 'Lord, Lord,' and do not do what I say?" (Luke 6:46). So spoke the One Christians call Master.

In the last eighteen years, as pastor of Philadelphia's Tenth Presbyterian Church, I have written thirty books. But I have not had apprehensions about how a book would be received until this one. I know that many will misunderstand it. They will suppose I am teaching that good works enter into a believer's justification — a false gospel. I am insisting on the full scope of Jesus' teachings about what being His disciple means. I stress obedience, service, humility, taking up the cross — all major themes in Christ's teaching. But I know because of the weaknesses and distortions of much of today's evangelical teaching that many will see this as somehow being something new and dangerous, and they will reject it as an alien gospel.

Only a few (but I am concerned for those few) will take Christ's call to discipleship seriously and profit by this study.

It is not unusual to hear about Christ's being Lord of all life and that we must acknowledge this if we are Christians. But those who understand what Christ's lordship actually means face a battle on two fronts. One front is manned by the world, which seeks to push Christians back onto the reservation. It says that believers can practice their religion there, where it will do no harm, but that they are not to think of bringing Christianity into the real world of politics, economics, law, and individual "rights." We must oppose this. We must declare that "the earth is the Lord's, and everything in it, the world, and all who live in it" (Psalm 24:1). We must show that "all authority in heaven and on earth" has been given to Jesus and indicate what this means (Matthew 28:18).

But the other front is equally challenging. It is held by well-intentioned but erring Christians who believe that it is possible to have Jesus as Savior without having Him as Lord and even go so far as to say that "lordship salvation," as they call it, is a false gospel. We who oppose this say that there is only one Savior, the *Lord* Jesus Christ, and that anyone who believes in a Savior who is not the Lord is not believing in the true Christ and is not regenerate. We call for commitment to Christ, the true Christ, and challenge the presumption that claims to be Christian while at the same time disregarding or disobeying Christ's commands.

It is Jesus who said, "If anyone would come after me, he must deny himself and take up his cross daily and follow me" (Luke 9:23).

It is Jesus who told the Jews of His day, "Unless your righteousness surpasses that of the Pharisees and the teachers of the law, you will certainly not enter the kingdom of heaven" (Matthew 5:20).

I believe that if America could produce a generation of Christians who genuinely affirm and live by these teachings, that generation by the power of God could transform the world.

In each of my books I thank those who have been particularly helpful to me in seeing the work through its early preaching stages and then into print. The first order of thanks goes to the congregation of Tenth Presbyterian Church, who support me in the use of my time for study, preaching, and writing. Second, I thank the many excellent people on the church staff who ably cover bases that I cannot cover, especially at this present period of significant growth for our center-city congregation. Finally, I thank my exceedingly able secretary, Caecilie M. Foelster, who carefully types and retypes my manuscripts and faithfully sees them through the various stages of proofreading and production. Since we are partners in this work, I know that she and the entire congregation join me in praying that these studies may be used of God as one of the many means needed to revive God's people and bring reformation to our land.

The Meaning of Discipleship

1

The Call to Discipleship

Follow me.   — Matthew 9:9

Come, follow me . . . and I will make you fishers of men.
                                        — Mark 1:17

If I want him to remain alive until I return, what is that to you? You must follow me.
                                        — John 21:22

There is a fatal defect in the life of Christ's church in the twentieth century: a lack of true discipleship. Discipleship means forsaking everything to follow Christ. But for many of today's supposed Christians — perhaps the majority — it is the case that while there is much talk about Christ and even much furious activity, there is actually very little following of Christ Himself. And that means in some circles there is very little genuine Christianity. Many who fervently call Him "Lord, Lord" are not Christians (Matthew 7:21).

We should not be surprised by this, because Jesus Himself said that this would be the case. But we should be distressed by it.

In Jesus' great sermon on the Mount of Olives, uttered shortly before His crucifixion, Jesus compared professing (but unconverted) Christians to women waiting for a bridegroom to appear for a wedding banquet. They were unprepared for his coming and were therefore shut out of the wedding. They were not saved. Again, Jesus compared professing Christians to a man who was given a talent to invest but who failed to use it and was condemned by his master on the day of reckoning. Jesus said that he was thrown "into the darkness, where there will be weeping and gnashing of teeth" (Matthew 25:30). In a third comparison He described these people as failing to feed the hungry, give drinks to those thirsting, receive strangers, clothe the naked, care for the sick, and visit those who were imprisoned. These people called Jesus "Lord." They considered themselves to be genuinely converted persons. But they were not Christians and so perished.

We need to see where this is true in our churches. We need to ask what it means to be a Christian and whether those shortcomings are descriptions of ourselves.

Costly Grace

There are several reasons that the situation I have described is common in today's church. The first is a *defective theology* that has crept over us like a deadening fog. This theology separates faith from discipleship and grace from obedience. It teaches that Jesus can be received as one's Savior without being received as one's Lord.

This is a common defect in times of prosperity. In days of hardship, particularly persecution, those who are in the process of becoming Christians count the cost of discipleship carefully before taking up the cross of the Nazarene. Preachers do not beguile them with false promises of an easy life or indulgence of sins. But in good times, prosperous times, the cost does not seem so high, and people take the name of Christ without undergoing the radical transformation of life that true conversion implies. In these times, preachers often delude them with an "easy" faith — Christianity without the cross — in order to increase the numbers on their church rolls, whether or not the added people are regenerate.

Dietrich Bonhoeffer, the German churchman of the Nazi era who eventually suffered martyrdom for his opposition to Hitler's policies, called this erroneous theology "cheap grace." He said, "Cheap grace is the preaching of forgiveness without requiring repentance, baptism without church discipline, communion without confession, absolution without personal confession. Cheap grace is grace without discipleship, grace without the cross, grace without Jesus Christ living and incarnate."

The contrast is "costly grace."

> Costly grace is the treasure hidden in the field; for the sake of it
> a man will gladly go and sell all that he has. It is the pearl of
> great price, to buy which the merchant will sell all his goods. It
> is the kingly rule of Christ, for whose sake a man will pluck out
> the eye which causes him to stumble; it is the call of Jesus Christ
> at which the disciple leaves his nets and follows him. Costly
> grace is the gospel which must be *sought* again and again, the
> gift which must be *asked* for, the door at which a man must
> *knock*. Such grace is *costly* because it calls us to follow, and it is
> *grace* because it calls us to follow *Jesus Christ*.[1]

Another writer, an American, bemoaned the same situation.
Chicago pastor and devotional author A. W. Tozer declared,

> The doctrine of justification by faith — a Biblical truth and a
> blessed relief from sterile legalism and unavailing self-effort —
> has in our time fallen into evil company and been interpreted
> by many in such manner as actually to bar men from the knowl-
> edge of God. The whole transaction of religious conversion has
> been made mechanical and spiritless. Faith may now be exer-
> cised without a jar to the moral life and without embarrassment
> to the Adamic ego. Christ may be "received" without creating
> any special love for him in the soul of the receiver. The man is
> "saved," but he is not hungry or thirsty after God. In fact he is
> specifically taught to be satisfied and encouraged to be content
> with little.[2]

It is not only a false theology that has encouraged this fatal lack
of discipleship. The error is also due to the absence of what the
older devotional writers called a "self-examined life."

Most Westerners live in a tragically mindless environment. Life
is too fast, and our contact with other persons too impersonal for
any real thought or reflection. Even in the church we are far more
often encouraged to join this committee, back this project, or
serve on this board than we are counseled to examine our relationship to God and His Son Jesus Christ. So long as we are perform-
ing for the church, few question whether our profession is genuine

---

1. Dietrich Bonhoeffer, *The Cost of Discipleship* (New York: Macmillan, 1966), p. 47.
   Original German edition 1937.
2. A. W. Tozer, *The Pursuit of God* (Harrisburg, Pa.: Christian Publications, 1948), pp.
   12-13.

or spurious. But sermons should suggest that members of a church may not actually be saved, although they are members. Teachers should stress that a personal, self-denying, costly, and persistent following of Christ is necessary if a person is to be acknowledged by Jesus at the final day.

In the absence of this teaching millions drift on, assuming that because they have made verbal acknowledgment of Christ ten, twenty, or even thirty years ago and have done nothing terribly bad since, they are Christians, when actually they may be far from Christ, devoid of grace, and in danger of perishing forever.

"FOLLOW ME"

In this book I want to examine what the Lord Jesus Himself said about discipleship. Study will range over a number of sayings that, taken together, show the meaning, path, cost, and rewards of this essential pursuit. But I say at the outset that the arguments of each of the following chapters are essentially one thesis, namely, that discipleship is not a supposed second step in Christianity, as if one first becomes a believer in Jesus and then, if he chooses, a disciple. From the beginning, discipleship is involved in what it means to be a Christian.

So I begin at square one, and the start of this area of Christian doctrine is Christ's command "Follow me." There are many texts in which Jesus explains in greater detail and with other images what it means to be His disciple, but the command to follow Him is the first and most basic explanation.

We find it in a number of stories, chiefly in the callings of the first disciples. In Matthew 4:18-22 (parallels in Mark 1:14-20 and Luke 5:1-11), we are told that Jesus was walking by the Sea of Galilee when He saw two brothers, Simon Peter and Andrew. Jesus said, "Come, follow me . . . and I will make you fishers of men." At once they left their nets and followed Him. He went a bit farther and saw two more brothers, James and John, sons of Zebedee. He called them in a similar manner, and they too left their boat and followed Him. Several chapters later in Matthew 9:9-13 (parallels in Mark 2:13-17 and Luke 5:27-32), there is an account of the call of Matthew, also named Levi. Matthew was a tax-collector. He was despised by the people for his collaboration with the Roman authorities. But he obeyed Christ and followed Him. When the people protested Jesus' association with this "sinner," Jesus replied, "It is not the healthy who need a doctor, but the sick. But go and learn what this means: 'I desire mercy, not sacrifice.' For I have not come to call the righteous, but sinners." This explanation shows that the command to follow Jesus was not understood by Him to be only a mere physical following or even an invitation to learn more about Him and then see if one wanted to be a permanent disciple or not. Jesus understood it as turning from sin to salvation. It was a call to healing by God.

The gospel of John does things differently from the Synoptics, but the call to follow Christ is no less prominent there. Indeed, there is a sense in which it provides a framework for the gospel. In chapter 1 there is a long narrative in which John the Baptist bears witness of Jesus as the Son of God and the Lamb of God. As a result, two of his disciples begin to follow Jesus physically. When Jesus sees them He issues the invitation, "Come" (v. 39), a synonym for "follow." Following Jesus is the theme of this chapter. Then, at the end of the gospel Jesus tells Peter, whom He has just recommissioned to service, "Follow me!" (John 21:19). When Peter shifts attention away from his own calling to ask about that of the beloved disciple, Jesus replies, "If I want him to remain alive until I return, what is that to you? You must follow me" (v. 22). Coming at the end of the gospel, these words are a statement to all would-be Christians that discipleship means following Jesus in a personal and generally costly way.

In all, the words "follow me" occur thirteen times in the gospels. But in addition there are scores of references in which one person or another is said to have followed Christ. Clearly it is a very basic concept.

Elements of Discipleship

In the course of this book each of the following elements will be considered in greater detail. But it is worth stressing here just how much is involved in the words "follow me."

1. *Obedience.* Obedience is an unpopular concept today that we betray by our frequent use of the phrase "blind obedience," meaning mindless adherence to authority. We think of it as enemy soldiers blindly carrying out the inhumane orders of an evil commander. So when we come to a phrase like "follow me" we naturally think of it as an invitation and conform our evangelism to that pattern. We "invite" people to follow Jesus, promising that He will receive them and make them happy. Well, there may be

an element of invitation in Christ's call to sinners, but the words "follow me" are in the imperative mood and are therefore a command — which is why those commanded to follow Jesus did in fact immediately leave their nets, boats, counting tables, or whatever else was occupying them and followed Jesus. On His lips the command "Follow me" was no more resistible than the command to Lazarus to "come out" (John 11:43). It was the equivalent of what theologians term God's "effective call."

That is another way of saying that without obedience there is no real Christianity. It is not that people cannot "follow" Jesus in a lesser sense and then fall away when the demands of genuine discipleship become clear to them. Many persons in the gospels seem to have done this. The rich young ruler is an example. But that is not the same as a sheep of Christ's flock hearing His call and responding to His voice as he recognizes Jesus as his Lord and Master. Those who are genuinely Christ's sheep obey His call from the beginning and enter into a life characterized by obedience.

2. *Repentance.* When Jesus called Matthew, He called one who was a recognized sinner. So He emphasized repentance: "I have not come to call the righteous, but sinners to repentance" (Luke 5:32). But the need for repentance is no less evident in the calls of the other disciples. For example, in both Matthew and Mark the account of the calling of the first disciples is immediately preceded by a record of Christ's first preaching, focusing on the words "Repent, for the kingdom of heaven is near" (Matthew 4:17; cf. Mark 1:14). In Luke's account the equivalent story is embedded in Jesus' first miraculous intervention in the disciples' fishing, where they caught so many fish the net was breaking. That story records Peter's profound experience of Christ's holiness and of his own sin that led him to cry out, "Go away from me, Lord; I am a sinful man!" (Luke 5:8). The point is that it is impossible to follow Christ without repentance.

How could it be otherwise? Jesus is the holy, sinless Son of God. He has never taken one step in any sinful direction. He has never led the way into a single sinful thought. So anyone who is following Him, not some imaginary Jesus, must by definition have turned his back upon sin and set his face toward righteousness. Christians do sin. When they do they must confess it and turn from it, being restored to fellowship again. But anyone who thinks he can follow Christ without renouncing sin is dreadfully confused. And anyone who claims to be following Christ while actu-

ally continuing in unrighteousness is deluded. And he or she is not
a Christian.

3. *Submission.* In one of Jesus' most important sayings about discipleship, which we will study more carefully in the next chapter,
the Lord pictures discipleship as putting on a yoke. This suggests a
number of things, but chiefly it suggests submission to Christ for
His assigned work. It is the picture of an animal yoked to others as
well as to a plow.

A yoke is also the connection between submission and subjec-
tion. "Submit" comes from the two Latin words *sub* (meaning
"under") and *mitto, mittere* (meaning "to put" or "place"). So submission means putting oneself under the authority of another.
"Subject" also comes from two Latin words, in this case *sub*
(meaning "under") and *iacto, iactare* (meaning "cast" or "throw").
It means being *put under* the authority of another. In other words,
although the first word has an active sense (I put myself under another's authority) and the second word has a passive sense (I am
placed under that authority), the idea is nevertheless essentially
the same. Moreover, it is connected with "yoke" in this way. In
ancient times it was customary for a ruler, when he had conquered
a new people or territory, to place a staff across two upright poles,
perhaps four feet off the ground, and require the captured people
to pass under it. By this act they passed under his yoke or submit-
ted to his authority. When Jesus used this image He was saying
that to follow Him was to submit to Him. It was to receive Him as
Lord of one's life.

4. *Commitment.* The fourth element in following Christ is commitment, for the simple reason that it is impossible to follow
Christ without being committed to Him. A lack of commitment
means deviating from His path or falling away from Him. On the
other hand, it is impossible to be committed to Christ without following Him, for a failure to follow really means being committed
to some other thing or person.

Surprisingly, this has become a hotly contested issue today on
grounds that teaching commitment to Christ is to add something
else to faith, which is a false gospel. This is the view, for example,
of Charles C. Ryrie, former dean of doctoral studies and professor
of systematic theology at Dallas Theological Seminary. He writes,
"The message of faith only and the message of faith plus commitment of life cannot both be the gospel; therefore, one of them is a

false gospel and comes under the curse of perverting the gospel or preaching another gospel (Galatians 1:6-9)."[3] Those who hold to this position do not deny that commitment is a good thing in and of itself or that it is necessary for growth in the Christian life. But they do deny that commitment stands at the beginning in the sense that one cannot really be saved without it. They would even take issue with a lordship of Christ expressed as *"willingness to commit one's life absolutely"* to Him, the implication being that it is possible to believe on Jesus as one's Savior from sin without willingness to follow Him.

Three arguments are advanced in support of the above line of thought. First, Scripture contains examples of believers who were not completely committed to Jesus and yet were saved. Peter resisted Christ's authority (Acts 10:14). Barnabas disagreed with Paul over whether they should take John Mark along with them on a second missionary journey (Acts 15:39). Certain believers at Ephesus apparently refused to give up their magic charms and books for as long as two years after they had become Christians (Acts 19). Lot was saved and was declared a righteous man by God even when he was living in Sodom (2 Peter 2:7-8).

The issue, however, is not whether believers sin. Obviously they do. It is whether they can come to Christ in faith while at the same time denying or resisting His lordship over them. It is that which is impossible.

A second argument is the meaning of the word *Lord.* It is reasoned that in reference to Jesus, *Lord* means "God Jesus" or "Jehovah Jesus." Since *Lord* means "Jehovah," all other meanings are excluded, according to this view. Particularly, it does not mean "Master." But *Lord* does mean Master. That is why a word that was originally used on the human level to denote one who is sovereign over slaves is used of God. Jehovah is called Lord because He *is* Master. He is the sovereign Master, hence, the *Kyrios* of which all other *kyrioi* are but shadows. Who is God if not Master? If God is not sovereign, He is not God. No other God than the sovereign God is presented to us in the Bible.

A third argument is the one suggested earlier, namely, that to insist on the lordship of Christ in salvation is to require something other than the work of Christ. It is to add works to faith, which is, as all true Christians confess, a false gospel. Dr. Ryrie seems to have this in mind as he concludes, "If you are ever tempted to add

---

3. Charles C. Ryrie, *Balancing the Christian Life* (Chicago: Moody, 1973), p. 170.

something to the uncomplicated grace of God, first try making it crystal clear who is the Object of faith and what is its content. Then point men to Him, the Lord Jesus, the God-Man Saviour who offers eternal forgiveness to all who believe."[4]

Yet that is precisely the point on which all true believers insist. We do not wish to add anything to Christ's finished work; it is for that very reason that we direct believers to the Lord Jesus Christ. But He is the *Lord* Christ. This Lord is the object of faith and its content. There is no other. Consequently, if faith is directed to one who is not Lord, it is directed to one who is a false Christ of the imagination. Such a one is not the Savior, and he will save no one.

Moreover, there is the meaning of faith itself. Is "faith" minus commitment a true biblical faith? We remember that the apostle James goes so far as to insist — in a passage some have erroneously thought contradicts the Pauline doctrine of justification by faith — that a faith without works is dead (James 2:17, 26). Such "faith" is useless (v. 20), worth nothing (v. 16). It is a claim to faith only (v. 14), not a genuine faith, which comes of God and expresses itself in works that please Him. But if that is true — if faith without works is dead — how much truer it is that faith without commitment is also dead. True faith involves these elements: *knowledge,* upon which it is based; *heart response,* which results from the new birth; and *commitment,* without which "faith" is no different from the assent of the demons who "believe . . . and shudder" (James 2:19). No one is saved by a dead faith. But a living faith is faith in Jesus as Lord and Savior, for the Lord is the Savior and the Savior is the Lord.

One must be appreciative of the concern Dr. Ryrie and those who think like him have to preserve the purity of the gospel. We agree wholeheartedly that any addition to the perfect work of Christ by sinful men and women perverts the gospel and is destructive to Christianity. If works enter into salvation in any way, those who trust in them are not saved by Jesus and are lost. All true Christians agree in that. But any attempt to divorce Christ as Savior from Christ as Lord also perverts the gospel, for anyone who believes in a Savior who is not the Lord is not believing in the true Christ and is not regenerate.

5. *Perseverance.* The final important element in following

4. Ibid., p. 181.

Christ is perseverance. This is because following is not an isolated act, done once and never to be repeated. It is a lifetime commitment that is not fulfilled here until the final barrier is crossed, the crown received, and it and all other rewards laid gratefully at the feet of Jesus.

Is salvation something that takes place in the past, something that is taking place now, or something that is to take place at the Lord's return? The answer is that all three are salvation and that isolating any one is an error fatal to the preservation of the gospel. Salvation took place in the past. So it is right to say that Jesus saved us by His death on the cross. His death redeemed His people. His blood made atonement for their sins. But this is not the only way the Bible speaks of salvation. It also speaks of a present element, of our "being saved" (1 Corinthians 1:18). Moreover, it looks forward to a time when by the continuing grace of God we will be saved utterly. With that blessed end in view it admonishes us to persevere in our commitment. Jesus said, "All men will hate you because of me, but he who stands firm to the end will be saved" (Matthew 10:22). Peter spoke of growth in godliness and concluded, "Therefore, my brothers, be all the more eager to make your calling and election sure. For if you do these things, you will never fall, and you will receive a rich welcome into the eternal kingdom of our Lord and Savior Jesus Christ" (2 Peter 1:10-11). Paul said, "Work out your salvation with fear and trembling, for it is God who works in you to will and to act according to his good purpose" (Philippians 2:12*b*-13).

All this is to say that discipleship is not simply a door to be entered but a path to be followed and that the disciple proves the validity of his discipleship by following that path to the very end. David wrote about it in Psalm 119. The section that begins, "Your word is a lamp to my feet and a light for my path," ends, "My heart is set on keeping your decrees *to the very end*" (vv. 105, 112, my emphasis). That is it! The true disciple follows Jesus to the end of everything.

WHOEVER WILL MAY COME

In the last years of the seventeenth century a French aristocrat wrote a book on discipleship that became a classic in the field. At one time the book was publicly burned in France. Yet it has been received by millions who have judged it one of the most helpful books ever written. It was loved by Fenelon, Count Zinzendorf,

John Wesley, and Hudson Taylor. This aristocrat was Madame Jeanne Guyon. Her book bears the title *Experiencing the Depths of Jesus Christ* (French title: *Le Moyen Court et Tres Facile de Faire Oraison*). As she wrote this classic, Madame Guyon had a high standard of discipleship in view, but at the same time she was aware that the call to follow Christ was not some circumscribed invitation to be delivered only to a special body of believers or to all believers only as a second step in their religious experience. On the contrary, it is the essence of faith, and the invitation to come to Christ as a disciple is for all. She wrote:

> If you are thirsty, come to the living waters. Do not waste your precious time digging wells that have no water in them. . . .
> If you are starving and can find nothing to satisfy your hunger, then come. Come, and you will be filled.
> You who are poor, come.
> You who are afflicted, come.
> You who are weighted down with your load of wretchedness and your load of pain, come. You *will* be comforted!
> You who are sick and need a physician, come. Don't hesitate because you have diseases. Come to your Lord and show him all your diseases, and they will be healed!
> Come.[5]

That is the invitation that Christ's call to discipleship holds for every person. To be a Christian is no light matter. It is a call to a transformed life and to perseverance through whatever troubles may arise. It may be the hardest thing anyone can do. Yet anyone can do it, with Christ supplying the necessary strength. In the end it is the only thing that really matters.

Will you take that path?

The Master is going before you. He is looking back at you with a most compelling gaze. He is saying, "Come!" He is commanding, "Follow me!"

5. Jeanne Guyon, *Experiencing the Depths of Jesus Christ* (Goleta, Ca.: Christian Books, 1981), p. 2. Original edition about 1685.

2

In the School of Christ

Come to me, all you who are weary and burdened, and I will give you rest. Take my yoke upon you and learn from me, for I am gentle and humble in heart, and you will find rest for your souls. For my yoke is easy and my burden is light.

— Matthew 11:28-30

In one form or another human knowledge has been passed on through the centuries. But when we think of schools as places for formal learning, we inevitably think of Greece and the program of study established by Plato in Athens. Plato was the first to offer a regular education extending over three or four years in a fixed place. Like Socrates, he began by selecting promising pupils from a public field (or gymnasium) on the outskirts of Athens. The field was called the Academy from the name of an athletic hero, Academus. Consequently, Plato's school became known as the Academy, even though it relocated to the garden of his house, which adjoined the gymnasium.

Plato passed his house to his successor, Speusippus, and he to his successor. So the Academy in Athens became the first endowed institution of learning. It continued to operate for nine hundred years.

Aristotle, a pupil of Plato for twenty years, set up a school of his own, choosing as his location another public gymnasium known as the Lyceum. It is interesting that from these two Greek institutions numerous countries have derived three important terms for a school. Germanic nations take their term from the playing field and call their basic school a *gymnasium.* Frenchmen call school a *lycée,* after the Lyceum. English-speaking nations call many of their schools *academies.* It is right to say that the origins of the educational establishment of the Western world (and other parts of the world too) can be traced to these Greek schools and that the many millions currently studying in a great variety of fields are the successors of those pupils.

But not nearly as many are in the school of Plato as are in the school of Jesus Christ. Jesus founded His school when He told those of His day, "Come to me, all you who are weary and burdened, and I will give you rest. Take my yoke upon you and learn from me, for I am gentle and humble in heart, and you will find rest for your souls. For my yoke is easy and my burden is light" (Matthew 11:28-30).

"Come to Me!"

The small paragraph from the end of Matthew 11 is one of the most important sections of the Bible. England's great evangelical bishop, J. C. Ryle, said, "There are few passages in the four gospels more important than this . . . few which contain in so short a compass, so many precious truths."[1] This is particularly true in respect to discipleship. These words are a call to discipleship — "Come to me" — but they are expressed by images designed to reinforce and expand the themes developed in the last chapter.

The first point expanded in these verses is the one with which the last chapter closed, namely, the invitation to people of all ages, nations, and personalities to come to Christ. It is important to emphasize this, because we have a tendency to think that discipleship is somehow much too hard a calling for most people and that the call is therefore only for a special, gifted class of Christians. Few people have trouble with the idea that they must confess their sin and believe on the Lord Jesus Christ as Savior. They may not do it; but if they decide to, doing so itself does not seem too hard in their opinion. It is quite different when they see that forsaking sin and cleaving to Jesus in saving faith is not the matter of a moment or a mere intellectual assent to certain "religious" propositions. When it is seen that belief also involves recognition of Christ's lordship over life and a commitment to Him that is to

1. J. C. Ryle, *Expository Thoughts on the Gospels: St. Matthew* (Cambridge: James Clarke, 1974), p. 116.

persist through whatever hardships life may bring — to the very end of life, to death, and then through death to glory — when that is perceived, discipleship suddenly seems quite weighty and the calling hard.

But it is precisely at this point that the universal offer must be stressed. For as I said in the last chapter, although following Christ is, in a certain sense, the hardest thing anyone can ever do, at the same time it is possible for everyone, because Christ provides His disciples with the will to persist in that calling. He indicates the broad scope of the offer when He says, "Come to me, *all* you who are weary and burdened" (v. 28, my emphasis).

But notice, it is for those who know they are burdened. This does not refer to mere physical weakness or to what we would call the burdens of a hard life, though it may include them. Chiefly it refers to a sense of sin's burden and the need of a Savior. The context of Matthew 11 makes this clear, for the earlier part of the chapter contains an account of the rejection of John the Baptist and Jesus by the Jewish masses, followed by a denunciation of Chorazin, Bethsaida, and Capernaum for their failure to repent at Jesus' preaching. After this Jesus said, "I praise you, Father, Lord of heaven and earth, because you have hidden these things from the wise and learned, and revealed them to little children. Yes, Father, for this was your good pleasure" (vv. 25-26). Little children are those who are childlike in their self-evaluation and in faith. They recognize their need of a Savior and are willing to abandon themselves to Christ as that Savior. They are the opposite of those who are mature in pride, assured that they can save themselves.

This is why periods of great movements of God's Spirit are also periods of great repentance. It is why we are not in such a period today. It is why ours is a paltry age.

Are you impressed by large numbers of professing Christians, regardless of the moral tone or spiritual usefulness of their lives? If so, you will think ours a great age, since, as the Gallup poll informs us, there are more than 50 million born-again Christians in the United States.

Are you impressed with large churches? If so, you will judge ours an age of exceptional spiritual blessing, for the twentieth century has seen development of the largest churches in history. In the United States, particularly in the West, churches of five, ten, or even fifteen thousand members are common.

Are you impressed with Christian organizations and institutions? If so, you will judge ours an extraordinary age. We have well-run, Madison-Avenue type organizations to do almost anything, including telling us what it is we should do. And they are successful.

Are you impressed with money? If so, you must be ecstatic today, since more money is being given to Christian causes than ever before in human history. Even the most liberal churches report annual gains in revenue, while their membership statistics decline.

But if you are looking for something else — if you are looking for a mature knowledge of God and real godliness in Christian people and are bemoaning the secular spirit and accelerating moral decadence of our time, even within fellowships of professing followers of the Lord Jesus Christ — then you must grieve for the state of today's church and sorrow for the lost. You must long for more true discipleship. Where discipleship is present, people are sensitive to sin and turn from it. They turn to Jesus where relief from sin's dreadful burden can be found. Are we experiencing revival today, since so many claim to have had a born-again experience? Not in my opinion. We are only in an age when religion has again become popular.

LEARNING JESUS CHRIST

To those who have become sensitive to sin and who are looking for deliverance Jesus issued a challenge in terms of spiritual learning. He said, "Take my yoke upon you and learn from me, for I am gentle and humble in heart" (v. 29). When Jesus called disciples to "follow" Him He was comparing Christianity to a path His followers were to walk, He going ahead of them. When He challenged disciples to "learn from me" He was comparing Christianity to a school in which He was to be both subject matter and teacher. This is the school of Christ in which every true believer has matriculated and in which a lifelong course of study is proscribed. In this school graduation is glorification, the day of death.

The King James Version of Matthew 11:29 translates the words "learn from me" as "learn of me," thus making Jesus the subject matter of the Christian's study rather than the teacher.[2] This variation exists because the Greek preposition *apo*, which occurs here, can mean several things, including "of" or "from," and English

2. The *New King James Version*, revision of 1979, uses the *New International Version* wording.

has no exactly comparable word. Translators must choose one idea or the other when actually each of the ideas is necessary.

The fundamental idea is *knowing Christ Himself*, in precisely the sense of John 17:3, where Jesus prayed to the Father, "This is eternal life: that they may know you, the only true God, and Jesus Christ, whom you have sent." This knowledge of the Father and the Lord Jesus Christ is salvation, or eternal life.

We must be careful to explain what we mean when we speak of knowing God in a saving way, however. For this is no mere intellectual knowledge of God, any more than saving faith is mere intellectual assent to certain truths. Knowing God is a complex matter. England's J. I. Packer has written a best-selling book, *Knowing God*, in which he analyzes knowing. He points out that even in human terms there is a difference between knowing about something, knowing something personally, and knowing a person. We can learn about things easily. For example, we can learn about the government of the United States from books. We can learn how the various branches of government relate to each other. We can learn how people are elected to the Senate or the House of Representatives. We can learn how bills are drafted, passed, and funded. This is important knowledge, particularly if a person is contemplating a career in government, but it is obviously quite different from the knowledge that comes from actually working in government on the Washington scene. A person who has done this might say, "I know *how* Washington operates," and mean a great deal more than merely saying he knows *about* it.

When we move from the knowledge of things or processes to people we obviously go a great deal further. For one thing, people are not always predictable. They react unexpectedly. They cover up what they are like. This means that it is possible to spend a great deal of time with a person and perhaps say at the end of that time, "I don't really know him at all." Getting to know another person depends on two things: ourselves, and whether we want to know the person and will spend time at it, and the other person, who must be willing to reveal himself to us. In fact, when we weigh those factors, the most important is clearly the other person's willingness to open up and disclose what he or she is like.

Now take the matter of knowing to the highest level and ask what it means to know God. It obviously involves these lower stages. We must know *about* God, and we must *experience* God. All this, particularly the latter, also depends on God's *willingness* to reveal Himself to us, which He does in nature, the Bible, and the interpretation of the Bible to our hearts and minds through the Holy Spirit. But there is an additional factor. We are sinful. God is holy. Therefore, the knowledge of God in this deepest, saving sense also always involves a knowledge of ourselves in our sin and our wonder at the greatness of the love of God extended to such sinful creatures.

Packer says, "Knowing God involves, first, listening to God's word and receiving it as the Holy Spirit interprets it, in application to oneself; second, noting God's nature and character, as his word and work reveal it; third, accepting his invitations, and doing what he commands; fourth, recognizing, and rejoicing in, the love that he has shown in thus approaching one and drawing one into this divine fellowship."[3]

This is why preaching that neglects to mention sin is not true preaching and why "experience" of God that does not leave the worshiper with a profound sense of his or her own sinfulness and an even greater sense of the love of God is no true experience. It is why we live in an age whose religious "health" is an illusion. Today we have preachers, well-known, highly successful preachers, who refuse to mention sin in their teaching — not because it is difficult to do or because they have trouble doing it, but because, in their judgment, people do not need to hear about such subjects. They believe people feel bad enough as it is. They need rather to be affirmed. Affirmed? People today hardly feel the weight of sin at all. Nothing they do is ever considered sinful. Will you maintain that such persons know God and are saved by God even if they make profession of it?

The second idea in the command "learn from me" is having *Jesus Christ as our teacher* in this school. It is the idea that the *New International Version* and *New King James Version* translators focus on in their rendering. How does Jesus teach us? We can understand how He taught in the days of His earthly ministry. Then He literally called disciples to follow after Him and instructed them as they traveled about together. Most of the words of Jesus in our gospels are from these teaching sessions. How does Jesus teach us now, when He is in heaven and we are on earth?

Jesus answered that clearly in John 14:25-26 and 16:13-14: "All this I have spoken while still with you. But the Counselor, the Holy Spirit, whom the Father will send in my name, will teach you all things and will remind you of everything I have said to you.

---

3. J. I. Packer, *Knowing God* (Downers Grove, Ill.: InterVarsity, 1973), p. 32.

. . . I have much more to say to you, more than you can now bear. But when he, the Spirit of truth, comes, he will guide you into all truth. He will not speak on his own; he will speak only what he hears, and he will tell you what is yet to come. He will bring glory to me by taking from what is mine and making it known to you." According to Jesus, the Holy Spirit would first lead the disciples to remember and record His teaching in what we call the New Testament. Then He would guide Christ's followers into increasing knowledge of the truth on the basis of that written revelation.

UNDER THE YOKE

In calling disciples to labor in His school, Jesus introduced a further image to explain the relationship of the disciple to Himself that He had in mind. It was the image of a yoke. A yoke is placed over the head and shoulders of a farm animal, such as an ox or horse, to enable it to work. But it is also a rod under which people were sometimes required to pass in order to show allegiance to a conqueror. "Yoke" is a rich word, embodying several important elements.

1. *Submission.* This idea was developed in the last chapter and flows naturally from the picture of people passing under a conqueror's yoke. But also involved is the concept of an animal submitting to its master's yoke and a scholar submitting to the academic discipline of a professor. When we come to Jesus Christ in salvation we come to Him as our Master, who will henceforth guide our lives, superintend our work, and direct our studies. The great Baptist preacher Charles Spurgeon saw "take my yoke" as meaning, "If you will be saved by me, I must be your Master and you must be my servant; you cannot have me for a Savior if you do not accept me for a Lawgiver and Commander. If you will not do as I bid you, neither shall you find rest to your souls."[4]

2. *Work.* The yoke placed upon the shoulders of a farm animal enables it to work. The yoke of Christ, placed upon the shoulders of His followers, undoubtedly has a similar purpose in their lives. It means that we are hitched to His team or enlisted in His service. We are soldiers in His army, builders of His temple, evangelists for His gospel, ambassadors of His kingdom.

4. Charles Spurgeon, "Rest for the Labouring" in *Metropolitan Tabernacle Pulpit,* vol. 22 (Pasadena, Tex.: Pilgrim Publications, 1971), p. 621.

This explains why Jesus was so willing to link a person's salvation to whether he or she performed in His service, as in the stories of the wise and foolish virgins, the men who had been given talents, and the division of the sheep and the goats. Those stories trouble some people, because they seem to be saying that salvation depends upon works — whether people are alert and waiting for Jesus when He returns, whether they use the talents He has given, whether they feed the hungry, give drinks to the thirsty, receive strangers, clothe the naked, care for the sick, or visit those who are in prison — and not upon simple faith in Jesus Christ as Savior. Salvation by works *is* a false gospel, as all true Christians know. These people would probably call these parables false teaching if they were not the words of Jesus Himself, found in Scripture.

But, of course, these stories are not teaching a false gospel. The parables ask merely whether a person belongs to Christ or not, which means has he or she taken on Christ's yoke. If a person has taken Christ's yoke, which he does when he believes on Christ (there is no separating the two), he will work for Christ. Conversely, if he does not work for Christ, he clearly has not taken on Christ's yoke and has not believed on Him or come to know Him savingly. Notice that it is not a question of how much we are able to do for Christ. In the story of the talents one man earned five talents, another only two. Both were saved. The question is whether a person has taken on the yoke. It is whether we are working for Christ or not.

3. *Companionship.* The third element in the image of a yoke is companionship, which is another way of saying that there are also others in Christ's school. It is possible to have a yoke for just one animal, as the yoke in the one-horse sleigh. But yokes generally fit over the heads of two animals so that the load is distributed and the pull balanced. I am glad that it is like that in Christ's school. The work is often hard; the hours are long. Many fingers make the work light.

There may be this thought also. When Jesus said, "Take my yoke upon you and learn from me," He may have been saying that the yoke is His in the sense that a yoke is a farmer's and that he needs to place it upon our shoulders. But it may also be that the yoke is His in the sense that He is wearing it too and is calling us to take our place beside Him for the work to be done. In view of the Bible's teaching elsewhere, I think this is the correct idea. We are "God's fellow workers" (1 Corinthians 3:9; 2 Corinthians 6:1). Jesus did promise to go with us "to the very end of the age" (Matthew 28:20). We are working with Christ, and there is no load for us that He Himself does not pull.

Matthew Henry wrote, "We are yoked to work, and therefore must be diligent; we are yoked to submit, and therefore must be humble and patient; we are yoked together with our fellow-servants, and therefore must keep up the communion of saints."[5]

An Easy Burden

When we think of being harnessed together with others in Christ's school it is possible to be discouraged, especially if we reflect that the work is hard and the course of instruction is unending. It is like entering upon a work study program in which there are no holidays and no summer vacations. Perhaps the Lord sensed this as He spoke, for He appended three powerful inducements to obey His call.

First, He portrayed Himself as a kind and humble Master. Most of us have been in schools where teachers were not kind or humble. Perhaps they were lazy and compensated for their laziness by overloading their students. Teaching fellows have made undergraduates research their theses for them. Perhaps they were bitter. Maybe they had hoped for a better spot on the faculty; then they had been passed over for promotion and so took it out on their students. Perhaps they were filled with thoughts of their own importance and thus could hardly stoop to explain themselves to one who was not quite so far along the academic road. A semester with a teacher like that can seem forever.

Jesus is not that kind of teacher. Jesus is "gentle and humble in heart" (v. 29). He is easy to approach, glad to be helpful. The very next chapter of Matthew quotes Isaiah 42:3, "A bruised reed he will not break, and a smoldering wick he will not snuff out" (Matthew 12:20).

Second, Jesus speaks of His yoke being "easy" and His burden "light" (v. 30). That is an interesting thing for Him to say, because to my knowledge it is the only place in Scripture (perhaps in secular literature as well, except for that influenced by Christ's own words) where a yoke is portrayed as easy, light, or desirable. In all other biblical instances a yoke is onerous. One illustration

5. Matthew Henry, *Matthew Henry's Commentary on the Whole Bible*, vol. 5, *Matthew to John* (New York: Revell, n.d.), p. 161.

comes from the early days of King Rehoboam. When Rehoboam ascended the throne after the death of his father, Solomon, the people asked, "Your father put a heavy yoke on us, but now lighten the harsh labor and the heavy yoke he put on us, and we will serve you" (1 Kings 12:4). Rehoboam replied, "My father made your yoke heavy; I will make it even heavier. My father scourged you with whips; I will scourge you with scorpions" (v. 14). As a result the people rebelled, and the nation was divided into a Northern and a Southern Kingdom. In a similar manner the New Testament speaks of a "yoke of slavery" (Galatians 5:1; 1 Timothy 6:1). Throughout the Old and New Testaments "breaking the yoke" means deliverance.

Jesus' yoke is not like that. The reason His yoke is different is that He is different. Yokes of human masters are hard, because human beings are hard. They are sinners who treat subjects in a sinful manner. The yoke of Jesus is an easy yoke, because He is "gentle and humble in heart." True, there is work to do; this is sometimes trying. But it is not like living a life of sin. It is easy compared to that. And it is a joy when it is difficult. We come closer to describing what is involved in Christ's service when we say that in serving Him we find liberty and that in taking on His yoke we find deliverance.

Third, Jesus speaks of rest for tired disciples. In fact, He speaks of two rests. There is a rest that is *given:* "Come to me all you who are weary and burdened, and I will *give* you rest" (v. 28, my emphasis). And there is a rest that is *found:* "Take my yoke upon you and learn from me, for I am gentle and humble in heart, and you will *find* rest for your souls" (v. 29, my emphasis). These rests correspond to two references to peace in Paul's writings: "peace with God," which is the result of justification (Romans 5:1), and the "peace of God," which is ours as we lay our concerns before Him (Philippians 4:6-7).

Jesus is all you or any other poor, struggling, burdened soul will ever truly need. So why struggle further in sin? You are laboring onward like Pilgrim, distressed at the burden on your back. No earthly master will ever lift that burden. Many will add to it. Most will ignore your plight since they have burdens of their own.

Turn from lesser masters to the great and good Master.

Turn from lesser teachers to Him who can teach true godliness and whose teaching will save your soul.

3

Taking Up the Cross

If anyone would come after me, he must deny himself and take up his cross daily and follow me. For whoever wants to save his life will lose it, but whoever loses his life for me will save it. What good is it for a man to gain the whole world, and yet lose or forfeit his very self? If anyone is ashamed of me and my words, the Son of Man will be ashamed of him when he comes in his glory and in the glory of the Father and of the holy angels.

— Luke 9:23-26

At the beginning of these studies I wrote that there is a fatal flaw in the professing church today: a lack of true discipleship. Discipleship is talked about, of course. There are books about it, particularly about what is called "discipling" other people. Words are not the problem. What is lacking is the thing itself. But what are we to say about this next theme: the need for self-denial, expressed as taking up the cross? In this area it is not only self-denial that is lacking; it is an area about which we do not even speak.

This would be puzzling to saints who lived before us. If they could observe us today, they would never understand how we can profess to follow Jesus and at the same time ignore self-denial, because to them self-denial would seem to be the very essence of what it means to be Christ's. Today some argue about the essential marks of the church. It is customary to speak about faithful preaching of the Word and faithful administration of the sacraments as marks. To these some would add church discipline.

What a shock it would be to many who stop at this point to learn
that Martin Luther, among others, considered *suffering* to be a
mark of the church and badge of discipleship. One of the memo-
randa drawn up in preparation for the drafting of the Augsburg
Confession, the chief doctrinal statement of the Lutheran com-
munions, defines the church as the community of those "who are
persecuted and martyred for the gospel's sake."[1] The definition
seems extreme to easygoing, materialistic Christians. But it is not
extreme in view of Christ's words to those whom He challenged to
come after Him. To these He said, "If anyone would come after
me, he must deny himself and take up his cross daily and follow
me" (Luke 9:23).

This is *the* "hard" saying of Jesus about discipleship. We can
perhaps handle the call to follow Him — particularly if we do not
think too deeply about what following Jesus Christ means. We can
perhaps even handle the thought of being in Christ's school and
taking on His yoke. That at least seems only to involve hard work.
But a cross? Self-denial? A cross means death — death to self
— and that is not an easy thought to contemplate. No one wants
to die. Yet that is what Jesus told each of His followers to do daily.

SELF-ESTEEM OR SELF-DENIAL?

Why do we not hear more about self-denial? It cannot be because the demand to take up the cross is an isolated saying in the
Bible. The theme is frequent. The command to "take up" or
"bear" the cross occurs five times in Christ's teaching (Matthew
10:38; 16:24; Mark 8:34; Luke 9:23; 14:27). Some of these passages actually strengthen Luke 9:23. Matthew 10:38 says, "Anyone who does not take his cross and follow me *is not worthy of me*"
(my emphasis). Luke 14:27 says, "Anyone who does not carry his
cross and follow me *cannot be my disciple*" (my emphasis). This last
text teaches that there is no salvation apart from cross-bearing.
Yet it is an extremely rare matter to hear any of these texts spoken
of forcefully.

Walter J. Chantry, pastor of a Reformed Baptist Church in Carlisle, Pennsylvania, is an exception to this. He has written a powerful book about cross-bearing entitled *The Shadow of the Cross:
Studies in Self-Denial.*[2] At the beginning of this book he too notes

---

1. Dietrich Bonhoeffer, *The Cost of Discipleship* (New York: Macmillan, 1966), pp. 100-
   101. Original German edition 1937.
2. Walter J. Chantry, *The Shadow of the Cross: Studies in Self-Denial* (Carlisle, Pa.: Banner
   of Truth, 1981).

today's neglect of these essential gospel elements and searches for explanations.

One explanation is the perversion of these doctrines in the past. Past periods of church history have witnessed fanatic bursts of asceticism in which peace with God or sanctification was thought to be found in cutting oneself off from most normal contacts with the world. Monasticism is illustrative of that. In the early church the first great monastic was Anthony. He lived in the desert in the area of the Red Sea where he eventually died in A.D. 356 at 105 years of age. For many years he lived in complete isolation from other people. Then there were anchorites. These men, like Symeon Stylites (the best known), lived on top of stone pillars and spent their time praying. Stylites remained on the top of a pillar seventy feet high for thirty years until his death in A.D. 459.

People today naturally shy away from such extreme withdrawal, but they do not note that this was an aberration. At best it was a form of world-denial that (in some forms) could be a call for some Christians, though not the majority. Self-denial is demanded of all.

A second explanation Chantry gives for today's lack of teaching about taking up the cross is the holiness movement, which speaks of self-denial as a step to "a second work of grace." It has been popularized by books that speak about "the surrendered life" or "the secret of a happy life." According to this teaching, the Christian begins by simple faith but then progresses to growth or happiness by learning to give up self for Jesus. This teaching has a striking, though generally unnoticed, similarity to monasticism in that it upholds two levels, or degrees, of Christianity. There is ordinary Christianity. Then there is a superior Christianity that is marked by self-surrender, self-denial, and discipleship.

In my judgment, the real reason why so many do not talk about self-denial and cross-bearing as essential ingredients of Christianity is that we just do not like these ingredients. We like having our sins forgiven, at least if excess sin is destroying our lives and weighing on our consciences. We like the promises of Christianity. We want to be told that God will heal broken relationships (especially if we do not have to do anything about them), resolve inner conflicts (if it does not require discipline), and prosper our work. Some forms of gospel preaching actually promise prosperity. We like that. But denial? Taking up a cross? Suffering? We dislike that teaching. A preacher who wants to see his church grow soon learns to stop talking about it. Instead he tells people things that will build their self-esteem.

So the cross is neglected, and professing Christians are allowed to go their own ways, live for self, and, at best, miss the fullness of the gospel. At the worst, they are encouraged to think they are saved when actually they may not be Christians at all.

SAYING NO TO SELF

One of the most important things to be said about Christ's stringent definition of discipleship in Luke 9:23 is that the elements He mentions cannot be separated from each other or even be made progressive steps in the Christian life. That should be obvious from the way Christ states His demand. If He had intended a progression, at the very least we would have expected Him to put "follow me" first, then the matter of self-denial, and perhaps lastly the matter of taking up His cross. But that is not what He does. Jesus first speaks of anyone who might want to come after Him or be His disciple, then He spells out what that coming after Him means. It entails: (1) self-denial, (2) taking up the cross, and (3) following. Moreover, as the following verses show, if a person rejects those elements of discipleship, he may be trying to "save his life" and "gain the world," but the result will be the losing of his very self. He will be rejected by Christ when He returns in glory with His holy angels.

As soon as we think about these terms it is evident why this is true. When we think about what it means to deny oneself, we are at once brought to the radical distinction between a God-oriented life and a life of unrepentant self-seeking or sin.

Self-seeking is the opposite of self-denial. It has been the essence of sin from the beginning. Self-seeking caused the fall of Satan. Isaiah describes Satan's fall in the fourteenth chapter:

> You said in your heart,
>   "I will ascend to heaven;
> I will raise my throne
>   above the stars of God;
> I will sit enthroned on the mount of assembly,
>   on the utmost heights of the sacred mountain.
> I will ascend above the tops of the clouds;
>   I will make myself like the Most High."
> But you are brought down to the grave,
>   to the depths of the pit.
>
>   (vv. 13-15)

The most noticeable feature of Satan's boast is the fivefold repetition of the words "I will." "*I will* ascend to heaven . . . *I will* raise my throne above the stars of God . . . *I will* sit enthroned on the mount of assembly. . . . *I will* ascend above the tops of the clouds . . . *I will* make myself like the Most High" (my emphasis). This is a sad but true expression of self-seeking. God had a will that included a proper, given place for Satan. But Satan was dissatisfied with that. He wanted to place himself first in the universe. God replied that he will be brought down to the pit.

This spirit has passed to our race through the fall of Adam. It is why the Bible describes us as self-seeking sheep: "We all, like sheep, have gone astray, each of us has turned to *his own way*" (Isaiah 53:6, my emphasis).

It is why Peter describes unregenerate persons as those who "follow *the corrupt desire of the sinful nature* and despise authority" (2 Peter 2:10, my emphasis).

It is why the prodigal son of Jesus' parable declared, "Father, give me *my share* of the estate" (Luke 15:12, my emphasis).

It is why Paul described the last days, saying, "People will be lovers of *themselves*" (2 Timothy 3:1, my emphasis).

The opposite of that destructive way of life, originating with Satan, is the path of self-denial marked by the Lord Himself in His submission to suffering. Paul writes,

> Your attitude should be the same as that of Christ Jesus:
> Who, being in very nature God,
>   did not consider equality with God something to be grasped,
> but made himself nothing,
>   taking the very nature of a servant,
>   being made in human likeness,
> And being found in appearance as a man,
>   he humbled himself
>   and became obedient to death — even death on a cross!
> Therefore God exalted him to the highest place
>   and gave him the name that is above every name,
> that at the name of Jesus every knee should bow,
>   in heaven and on earth and under the earth,
> and every tongue confess that Jesus Christ is Lord,
>   to the glory of God the Father.
>
> (Philippians 2:5-11)

Satan said, "I want my way. I am going to displace God; I will rule the universe." God said that Satan would actually be brought low. Jesus said, "I will go down in self-denial. I will abase Myself in order that others, those I love, might be lifted from sin to glory." As a result, God promised that Jesus Christ would be exalted. He would be given that name which is above every name. Every tongue will confess that "Jesus is Lord."

SAYING YES TO GOD

But it is not only that we are to say no to self, which is what denying self is all about. We are also to say yes to God, which is what taking up the cross involves. Some speak of cross-bearing as if it means enduring the inevitable. But that is not it at all. There are all kinds of things that cannot be avoided: a physical handicap, a deficient academic background, a drunken husband, a profligate wife. People sometimes refer to such inevitable things as "my cross," but they are not crosses. They are just inescapable limitations, trials. Real crosses involve the will. They mean saying yes to something for Jesus' sake.

Cross-bearing involves prayer and Bible study. These take time and must be chosen and pursued, rather than other pastimes that we might humanly prefer.

Cross-bearing involves the items Jesus listed in Matthew 25:31-46 — feeding the hungry, giving drink to the thirsty, receiving the stranger, clothing the naked, caring for the sick, and visiting the one who is in prison. These are not easy things to do. They involve denying oneself time, money, and convenience. At times these efforts seem utterly fruitless, because the gifts are abused, and the one giving them is slighted even by the one he helps. We are to continue in this anyway. Doing so is saying yes to Jesus.

Cross-bearing involves witnessing. It means putting oneself out for the sake of the ones God sends into our lives.

Essentially, cross-bearing means accepting whatever God has given us or made us and then offering it back to Him, which is "your reasonable service" (Romans 12:1, KJV*). That phrase from Romans 12 is in a passage that describes us as God's priests making sacrifices that are "holy and pleasing" to Him. What is it that priests offer? They offer only what they have first received. They take the gifts of the worshiper and then offer them up. You and I are in that position. The gifts we receive are from God. We take these gifts — whatever they may be — and then offer them up to God with thanksgiving.

*King James Version.

The Demands of Cross-Bearing

The idea of a cross itself indicates what cross-bearing involves. Walter J. Chantry, whom I mentioned earlier, presents the demands of cross-bearing. I draw on his outline.

1. *The demand to take up the cross is universal.* In previous chapters, when I spoke about the offer of the gospel to people of every conceivable type and background, I spoke of a "universal" offer. But that is not the sense in which I use the word here. The universal offer of the gospel means that the way of salvation is offered to everybody so that "whoever wishes" may come to Christ (Revelation 22:17). Not all come; in fact, only those whom the Father draws come to Jesus (John 6:37, 44). But all may. Salvation is a universal offer. When we say that the demand to take up the cross is universal we mean something different. This demand is for all who follow Christ. So "universal" in this sense means that all who follow Christ and are therefore saved *must be* cross-bearers. That is, it is impossible to be a Christian without self-denial. The only way to avoid the cross is to follow the devil's self-seeking path and perish with him in hell.

Chantry writes:

> It is this most obvious aspect of our Lord's teaching which has been forgotten or ignored by modern evangelism. Anxious to bring sinners to life, peace and joy in the Lord, evangelists have failed even to mention that Christ insists upon denial of self at the outset. Having failed to pass on our Lord's requirement, and forgetting it themselves, evangelists have never questioned whether their "converts" with self-centered lives are true followers of Christ. Assuming that it is possible for a man to be self-in-dulgent and yet heaven bound, Bible teachers look for some way to bring egocentric men to a higher spiritual plane. Then self-denial is taught as the requirement for a second work of grace. . . .
>
> Those who save texts demanding a cross for "the deeper life" have cheated their hearers in evangelism. Without a cross there is no following Christ! And without following Christ there is no life at all! An impression has been given that many enter life through a wide gate of believing on Jesus. Then a few go through the narrow gate of the cross for deeper spiritual service. On the contrary, the broad way without self-denial leads to destruction. All who are saved have entered the fraternity of the cross.[3]

3. Ibid., pp. 21, 22.

2. *The demand to take up our cross is perpetual.* This point is similar to what I wrote in chapter 1. Only it is stronger. Earlier I said that following Christ requires perseverance for the reason that discipleship is not simply a door to be entered but a path to be followed. Having entered upon that path, the disciple proves the validity of his discipleship by pursuing it to the very end. Taking up the cross is like that. But when Jesus uses the word "daily," saying, "take up your cross *daily* and follow me," He is saying something stronger in that the cross must be taken up afresh each day.

When we turn our backs on our past to follow Christ, that is indeed taking up the cross. Having started out in that way, we must keep on. There is to be no turning back to bury a father or mother, purchase a piece of property, or whatever. But in addition to that, taking up the cross is also consciously to take up the self-denials and opportunities for serving others that each day brings. Chantry says, "Bearing a cross is every Christian's daily, conscious selection of those options which will please Christ, pain self, and aim at putting self to death. It is a teaching for the recruit, not merely for the seasoned warrior."[4]

3. *Taking up our cross is intentional.* This is the point I made earlier when I spoke of saying no to self in order that we might say yes to God. It is implied in Christ's command: "If anyone would come after me, he must deny himself and take up his cross daily and follow me." No one may take up the cross for you. A grandmother cannot take it up. A husband cannot take it up. Your children cannot take it up. You must do it. Furthermore, you must do it willingly. True, God must make you willing, for none of us is willing of himself. But when God worked upon us so that what we cherished before we now repudiate, and what we despised before we now cherish — when He has done that, it is then of our own free will that we take up our cross and follow Jesus. The soldiers of Christ are not slaves. They are freed men and women who count His service their greatest joy.

4. *Taking up our cross daily is painful.* In Jesus' day crosses were not the beautiful, polished, gold and silver ornaments we frequently see today. They were made of rough wood crudely shaped. To pick up a cross hurt the hands. To carry it on one's back meant working the splinters of the wood into the skin of one's shoulders.

4. Ibid., p. 25.

There was nothing pretty about a cross. A cross hurt. So does Christian service — at times. A moment ago I wrote that Christians count it joy to be engaged in Christ's service, and that is true. Nothing must detract from that. But that joy is often found in pain, just as with Jesus, "who for the joy set before him endured the cross, scorning its shame" (Hebrews 12:2). The same text says that we are to run that race, having our eyes set on Christ as our example.

5. *A cross is mortal.* That is, it has one purpose and one purpose only — to put the crucified one to death. Death on a cross is a slow death, but it is a certain one: "death to self-importance, self-satisfaction, self-absorption, self-advancement, self-dependence. . . . Death to self-interest because you serve Christ's honor!"[5]

Dietrich Bonhoeffer, who died for his commitment to Christ, understood this principle. He wrote,

> As we embark upon discipleship we surrender ourselves to Christ in union with his death — we give over our lives to death. Thus it begins; the cross is not the terrible end to an otherwise God-fearing and happy life, but it meets us at the beginning of our communion with Christ. When Christ calls a man, he bids him come and die. It may be a death like that of the first disciples who had to leave home and work to follow him, or it may be a death like Luther's, who had to leave the monastery and go out into the world. . . . Jesus' summons to the rich young man was calling him to die, because only the man who is dead to his own will can follow Christ. In fact, every command of Jesus is a call to die, with all our affections and lusts. . . . Every day [the Christian] encounters new temptations, and every day he must suffer anew for Jesus Christ's sake. The wounds and scars he receives in the fray are living tokens of this participation in the cross of his Lord.[6]

OUR EYES ON JESUS

The third part of Christ's description of discipleship in Luke 9:23 is the command "Follow me." We looked at that carefully in chapter 1, but now the challenge comes in a slightly different way. Having spoken of self-denial and cross-bearing, which the first two points of this text present, we find ourselves looking about for

5. Ibid., p. 25.
6. Bonhoeffer, p. 99.

some motivation that will bring us to that commitment. Knowing that the alternative is to lose our life or forfeit our very self helps. But the cost still seems high. In most cases, the only thing that will ultimately get us going along this path of self-denial and discipleship is following after Jesus, which means setting our eyes on Him as He has gone before us.

Jesus is the model for our self-denial. He is the image of cross-bearing.

Seeing this was the turning point in the life of Count Zinzendorf, the founder of the Moravian fellowships. In a little chapel near his estates in Europe there was a remarkable picture of Jesus Christ. The artist was a true child of God, and he had painted love for Christ and the love of Christ into his portrait as few have done either before or since. Underneath it were the lines, "All this I did for thee; what hast thou done for me?"

One day Zinzendorf entered the chapel and was arrested by the portrait. He recognized the love of Christ that had been painted into the face of the Master. He saw the pierced hands, the bleeding forehead, the wounded side. He read the couplet, "All this I did for thee; what hast thou done for me?" Gradually a new revelation of the claim of Christ on his life came upon him. He was unable to move. Hours passed. As the day waned the lingering rays of sunlight fell upon the bowed form of the young nobleman who was now weeping out his devotion to Him whose love had conquered his heart. Zinzendorf left that chapel a changed man. He went to work through the Moravians, whose missionary interests and Christlike service have encircled the globe.

That is what moves a person to follow after Jesus in the path of denial. It is what moves one to be a Christian in the first place — not the promise of rewards (though there are rewards) or an escape from hell (though following Christ does mean deliverance from hell). We are moved by the love of Jesus, for which He endured the cross.

People won by that love will never cease following after Jesus.

They "make every effort to enter through the narrow door" (Luke 13:24).

The Path of Discipleship

4

The Path of Obedience

Why do you call me, "Lord, Lord," and do not do what I say? I will show you what he is like who comes to me and hears my words and puts them into practice. He is like a man building a house, who dug down deep and laid the foundation on rock. When a flood came, the torrent struck that house but could not shake it, because it was well built. But the one who hears my words and does not put them into practice is like a man who built a house on the ground without a foundation. The moment the torrent struck that house, it collapsed and its destruction was complete.

— Luke 6:46-49

After the first three chapters of this book with their emphasis upon self-denial, submission, and perseverance in following Jesus Christ as a disciple, you may be feeling like a girl who talked to me after I had preached on cross-bearing. She had the idea that if she took what I said seriously, she would have to stop doing everything she enjoyed. She liked her job; she would have to give that up. She had friends she was comfortable with; she would have to drop them. She was thinking that the only way she could deny herself and take up her cross and follow Jesus was if she went off to some remote region of the world and served God "miserably" as a missionary.

The girl was on the wrong track, of course — as you may be if you are having similar thoughts. But it was not a simple matter to answer her. On the positive side there is a good chance that God will not want her to do anything of the sort. If the Lord has given her abilities that she is using in a worthwhile job, which she shows by her enjoyment of it, and if He has given her supportive Christian friends, there is a high probability that in the foreseeable future at least He will want her to stay right where she is. Taking up a cross is not intended to make anyone miserable, and in any case it probably has very little to do with quitting one's job and going off to a foreign country as a missionary.

On the other hand, it is possible that the Lord could lead in that way. Her job might not be the right job, even though she now enjoys it, and her present friends might not be God's final plan for her life.

One thing I told her is that God is full of surprises. It is what we should expect just by looking at the universe. Nature surprises us by sudden bursts of beauty, by the wise and sometimes humorous behavior of animals, by the action of sub-atomic particles, by black holes, quarks, and quasars. Following the Lord Jesus Christ as His disciple may be puzzling at times, even difficult. But it is not dull. Christians are sometimes disciplined by God, but their life with God is much closer to being a grand adventure than a punishment.

Another thing I told her is that discipleship nevertheless involves obedience. Obedience? Right here many people's antennae go up, and they become worried. Obedience does not fit their idea of what is adventuresome or fun. Obedience sounds like the army. Adventure? Well, that is like sailing a boat around the world with no time limits and no agenda. Actually, a vacation free from time limits can be pretty dull, as people who have tried it testify, and an obedient, disciplined life can be enjoyable. In our contemporary world there are probably no more disciplined and instinctively obedient men and women than astronauts, military personnel, and scientists. Yet what an adventure they have walking on the moon or planning to build and operate a space laboratory!

PROFESSION WITHOUT PRACTICE

Jesus was not thinking about adventure when He spoke of obedience in Luke's version of the Sermon on the Mount. He was thinking of a life able to produce the fruit of good works and righteousness or a life able to stand against life's tempests (Luke 6:43-49). But in speaking of obedience He was certainly emphasizing its importance and establishing it as an essential element in the

Christian life. Apparently He had been followed by people who
made verbal profession of discipleship. They called Him "Lord,"
which means that they were calling Him their Master and were
putting themselves forward as His servants. But they were disregarding His teaching. Jesus showed the impossibility of this intrin-
sic contradiction by asking pointedly, "Why do you call me,
'Lord, Lord,' and do not do what I say?" (v. 46). Jesus cannot be
our Lord without obedience; and if He is not our Lord, we do not
belong to Him. We are like a man whose house will be swept away
by a flood.

What a great problem this is — profession without practice!
And what a disaster! It has been a problem all through biblical
history.

It was true in Israel. On the day before the prophet Ezekiel
learned of the fall of the city of Jerusalem to the Babylonians, God
appeared to him to explain why this was happening. The explanation was in terms of the people's empty profession. God told Ezekiel, "Your countrymen are talking together about you by the
walls and at the doors of the houses, saying to each other, 'Come
and hear the message that has come from the Lord.' My people
come to you, as they usually do, and sit before you to listen to your
words, but they do not put them into practice. With their mouths
they express devotion, but their hearts are greedy for unjust gain.
Indeed, to them you are nothing more than one who sings love
songs with a beautiful voice and plays an instrument well, for they
hear your words but do not put them into practice" (Ezekiel 33:30-
32). Ezekiel teaches us that Jerusalem was destroyed because the
people were merely entertained by God's words and did not obey
them.

Isaiah said the same thing in words Jesus later quoted to His disciples, "The Lord says: 'These people come near to me with their
mouth and honor me with their lips, but their hearts are far from
me' " (Isaiah 29:13).

Jesus used this text to reprove teachers of the law who made a
profession of adhering to God's words when actually they were
obeying only man-made regulations. He called them "hypocrites"
and "blind guides" (Matthew 15:1-14; cf. Mark 7:1-16).

The problem of profession without practice was present in the
early Christian community, as proved by the epistle of James.

> Do not merely listen to the word, and so deceive yourselves. Do
> what it says. Anyone who listens to the word but does not do

what it says is like a man who looks at his face in a mirror and, after looking at himself, goes away and immediately forgets what he looks like. But the man who looks intently into the perfect law that gives freedom, and continues to do this, not forgetting what he has heard, but doing it — he will be blessed in what he does. (James 1:22-25)

There is nothing so obvious as the truth that in religion, words without practice are worthless, even contemptible. Yet few things are so common. One commentator writes, "Open sin, and avowed unbelief, no doubt slay their thousands. But profession without practice slays its tens of thousands."[1] It is what Jesus had in mind when He said that those who call Him "Lord, Lord," but do not obey Him will be carried away by life's torrents.

How Does Jesus Speak?

Thus far in this chapter we have made two points: that obedience is essential to the adventure of the Christian life as well as to discipleship (which is actually the same thing) and that lack of obedience is quite common. But assuming that you are interested in this adventure and are willing to obey Jesus and not just mouth religious words, the question nevertheless remains: How do you know what Jesus wants you to do? Should you leave your job or stay with it? Should you be an astronaut or a missionary? How does Jesus speak? How does He exercise His proper lordship in your life?

Several years ago, when I was in northern California, I turned on the radio and heard part of an unusual religious program. It was called "Have You Had a Spiritual Experience?" It was conducted as a call-in talk show. A phone number was given, and listeners were invited to describe their "spiritual experience" over the air.

While I listened, two people told their stories. The first was a girl who explained that she had felt a sudden urge to leave her home in northern California and hitchhike down the coastal road to a place about midway between San Francisco and Los Angeles. When she reached that midpoint, she sensed that "this was the place." So she got out of the car, went down the hill to the shore, found a cave where she camped out for two or three days, and communed with nature. She got into the water and swam about

1. J. C. Ryle, *Expository Thoughts on the Gospels: St. Luke*, vol. 1 (Cambridge: James Clark, 1976), p. 195.

among the rocks and seaweed as if she were alone at the dawn of creation. Then an animal came by and went off in a certain direction, and she took this as a "sign" that it was time to go. She climbed back up the hill and hitchhiked home. That was her experience.

The other person told this story. A short while before — on the first Tuesday of November 1980 — Americans went to the polls to choose Ronald Reagan over Jimmy Carter as President of the United States. She said that she had always been a Democrat. "I went into that booth planning to vote for Carter. But something happened. A strange feeling came over me, and I pulled the lever for Reagan." She did not say whether she thought this experience was of God or the devil, but I think she believed it was the latter — since she was a Democrat.

Is this the way God speaks to people? By feelings? Intuition? Is this the way the Lord Jesus Christ exercises lordship over His disciples?

This matter was of great concern to the Protestant Reformers, for they lived in a day when very few people had a sense of a true word from God and were instead burdened by what were only the traditions of the church. Or if they claimed to have received a true word from God, it was often supposed to have come through dreams, trances, sudden movings of the Holy Spirit, or personal intimations. Against these errors the Reformers stressed two things: (1) the Bible and (2) the work of God's Spirit illuminating the Bible. These worked together. The Reformers saw that God does not speak to a person through one without the other.

The Reformers were not dry rationalists. Luther, Calvin, and the others had faith in the power of the Holy Spirit to convert men and women, interpret the Word to them, and lead them spiritually. They believed this because the Bible has so much to say about it. The Bible says, "The wind blows wherever it pleases. You hear its sound, but you cannot tell where it comes from or where it is going. So it is with everyone born of the Spirit" (John 3:8). "The Spirit . . . testifies, because the Spirit is the truth" (1 John 5:6). "We have not received the spirit of the world but the Spirit who is from God, that we may understand what God has freely given us. This is what we speak, not in words taught us by human wisdom but in words taught by the Spirit, expressing spiritual truths in spiritual words. The man without the Spirit does not accept the things that come from the Spirit of God, for they are foolishness to him, and he cannot understand them, because they are spiritually discerned" (1 Corinthians 2:12-14). The reformers were Spirit-oriented men.

But at the same time, when they thought of these verses with their strong emphasis upon the Holy Spirit's revealing the ways and will of God, the Reformers also remembered other verses that stressed the importance of the Scriptures. So they said with equal emphasis that it is only through the Bible that God speaks.

Without the Holy Spirit the Bible is a dead book. That is why a person "without the Spirit" cannot understand it. In order to understand the Word, hear the voice of Christ in it, and begin to follow Him in obedience, the individual must be born again. In addition, he must wait on God and pray for the Holy Spirit's guidance. On the other hand, without the written Word of God as an objective guide, claims to a special leading of the Spirit quickly deteriorate into the kind of foolishness heard on the "Have You Had a Spiritual Experience?" program.

LIVING IN THE BOOK

Everything I have been saying so far leads to a practical conclusion, and it is this. If the adventure of discipleship involves obedience to Jesus Christ, as it certainly does, and if Jesus exercises His lordship over us so that we can obey Him through the Bible, as we have seen to be the case, then there can be no real discipleship apart from Bible study. Bible study is no option for Christians. It cannot even be a minor, occasional, or "vacation time" pursuit. Bible study is the most essential ingredient in the believer's spiritual life, because it is only in study of the Bible as that is blessed by the Holy Spirit that Christians hear Christ and discover what it means to follow Him.

If you have been called by Christ and therefore sincerely want to hear His voice as He speaks to you through the Bible, you should do the following.

1. *Study the Bible daily* (Acts 17:11). We can study the Bible more than once each day, of course. There may be days when legitimate concerns consume the time we would normally spend studying. But we should discipline our lives to include a normal, daily period of Bible study, just as we discipline ourselves to have regular periods for sleep, brushing our teeth, meals, and so on. In fact, the comparison with regular mealtimes is a good one, for these are necessary if the body is to be healthy and good work is to

be done. On occasion we may miss a meal, but normally we should not. In the same way, we must feed regularly on God's Word if we are to become and remain spiritually strong.

What happens if we neglect such daily Bible reading? We grow indifferent to God and lax in spiritual things. We throw ourselves open to temptation and the sin that easily follows.

The regular time we set aside for Bible study may be long — for those who are mature in faith and who have time for such study, perhaps an hour or two, even more. It may be shorter — for those who are new in faith or who lead tight schedules, perhaps only ten or fifteen minutes. Whatever the length of time, it should be fixed and at a set period of the day.

When should this be? Again, this may vary from person to person. Many have found that the best time is at the very beginning of the day. R. A. Torrey wrote,

> Whenever it is possible, the best time for this study is immediately after rising in the morning. The worst time of all is the last thing at night. Of course, it is well to give a little while just before we retire to Bible reading in order that God's voice may be the last to which we listen, but the bulk of our Bible study should be done at an hour when our minds are clearest and strongest. Whatever time is set apart for Bible study should be kept sacredly for that purpose.[2]

2. *Study the Bible systematically* (Joshua 1:7-8). Some people read the Bible at random, dipping here or there. This may be characteristic of the way they do most things in life, but it is a mistake in Bible study. It leads to a lack of proportion and depth, which is often characteristic of American Christians. A far better system is a regular, disciplined study of certain books of the Bible or even of the Bible as a whole.

New Christians should begin with one of the gospels, perhaps the gospel of John or Mark. After that they should study Acts, Ephesians, Galatians, Romans, or an Old Testament book like Genesis. It is always valuable to meditate on the Psalms.

Certain procedures should be followed during study. First, the book itself should be read through carefully as many as four or five times, perhaps one of these times aloud. Each time something new will strike you.

2. R. A. Torrey, *How to Succeed in the Christian Life* (Westwood, N. J.: Revell, 1906), p. 50.

Second, divide the book into its chief sections, just as we divide modern books into chapters (not necessarily the same chapters as in our Bibles), subsections, and paragraphs. At this stage the object should be to see which verses belong together, what subjects are covered, and the sequence of the subjects.

Third, these sections should be related to one another. Which are the main sections or subjects? Which are introductory? Which make applications? At this stage, one should be developing an outline of the book and should be able to answer such questions as: What does this book say? To whom was it written? Why was it written? If you were studying Romans, for example, you should be able to say, "This book was written to the church at Rome, but also to churches in all places and at all times. It says that we are lost in sin and that the answer to that sin is the righteousness of God revealed in Jesus Christ. Its purpose is to explain the gospel. A minor purpose was to alert the Romans to Paul's desire to visit them on his way to a future ministry in Spain."

You can now proceed to a more detailed study of the sections. What is the main subject of each section? What is said about it? Why is it said? To whom? What are the conclusions that follow from it? It is helpful to watch the small connecting words like *but*, *because*, *then*, *and*, *since*, and *therefore*.

Last, you can study key words. Begin by looking at other passages in the same book in which the word occurs. You can find these by your own reading or by using a concordance in which verses containing a given word are listed. Simple concordances are in the backs of many Bibles.

Suppose you were studying Romans 3:21-26 and wanted to learn more about the important word *righteousness*, with which the section begins. One key verse is 10:3, in which the righteousness of God is distinguished from our righteousness. Also, Romans 1:17 says that the righteousness of God is made known in the gospel. In all, *righteousness* is used thirty-five times in this one letter alone, and most of these uses throw light on one another. At this point you may also observe the use of the word in other books of the Bible, perhaps using the chain-reference system that some Bibles provide. You can also use an English dictionary. Some large dictionaries contain the derivations of words, which also throw light on their meanings.

3. *Study the Bible comprehensively* (2 Timothy 3:16-17). Alongside study of one book or section of the Bible, there should be an

attempt to become acquainted with the Bible as a whole. This means reading it comprehensively. True, many parts of the Bible will not appeal to us at first. That is natural. But if we never make an attempt to become acquainted with them, we limit our growth and may even warp our understanding. Paul told Timothy, "*All* Scripture is God-breathed and is useful for teaching, rebuking, correcting and training in righteousness" (2 Timothy 3:16, my emphasis). Jesus will speak to you and tell you what to do, not only in the red-ink portions of those Bibles that indicate His own words, but in many portions of Scripture.

4. *Study the Bible devotionally* (Psalm 119:11). There is a danger when we speak of daily, systematic, and comprehensive Bible study of encouraging a person to think that such study is therefore mechanical and can be pursued in the same manner as one would study a secular text. That is not the case. The Bible is not like other books that have been written by men or women and therefore contain part truth and part error and that at best only touch us on the human level. The Bible is written by God and is therefore infinitely superior to all other publications. The purpose of our study is also different. In other books we study to become wise. In reading the Bible we study to know God, hear His voice, and be changed by Him through our obedience as we grow in holiness. The attitude of the student must also be different. We can approach other books pridefully, perhaps considering ourselves wiser or more knowledgeable than the persons who wrote them. We must approach the Bible humbly and with childlike faith. We must wait upon Jesus. Our prayer must be the prayer the aged Eli taught Samuel, "Speak, Lord, for your servant is listening" (1 Samuel 3:9).

Also, if we really want the Bible to become a part of us so that the mind of Christ, which is expressed in the Bible, becomes our mind, then we must memorize sections of Scripture. Our educational system does little to stress memorization today. But those who were educated a generation ago will testify that what they memorized then, whether simple verse or more complex passages from Shakespeare or another distinguished writer, have remained with them and have thereby become a part of what they are. That is what we need as Christians. We need to allow the Word of God to become a part of us. To have that happen we must memorize it.

I have a friend who has an extremely busy schedule and who is under great pressures in his job. Nevertheless, he faithfully spends

twenty minutes a day in uninterrupted Bible study and in addition
to that spends whatever time is necessary to memorize one verse
each day. He has memorized a verse each day for five years, and he
testifies that this is the single most important factor in his discipleship and spiritual growth.

5. *Study the Bible prayerfully* (Daniel 9:1-3). It is impossible to
study the Bible devotionally without praying, since we are coming
to God in Scripture and must communicate with Him verbally if
we do. But although prayer is a part of a devotional study of Scripture, prayer is worth stressing for its own sake, if only because we
so often neglect it. The best way to study the Bible is to encompass
our study in prayer. Before we begin we should quiet our hearts,
saying, "I am about to study the book that God has given me. In
that book I am going to meet Him and hear the voice of my Savior, the Lord Jesus Christ. What I hear, I want to obey." Then
having quieted our hearts, we should turn to God Himself and
pray, "Lord God, I am turning to Your Word. By myself I cannot
understand it as I should. I need the Holy Spirit to instruct me and
draw a proper response from me. What I understand I want to
obey. Help me to do that for Jesus' sake." We must then study the
passage for the day, and as we find something that pertains directly
to us, we must stop again and acknowledge that prayerfully. We
must say, "Lord God, I know You are speaking to me in this passage. I am beginning to understand what You want me to do. Help
me do it as soon as possible, and make this principle a part of my
mind and behavior so that when other situations of this kind
emerge I will respond to them as this passage tells me I should and
live more like Jesus Christ."

Without regular, personal Bible study and prayer, we are not
really walking with Christ as His followers, and we are certainly
not obeying Him in specifics.

THE LIBERTY OF OBEDIENCE

But suppose we do pursue regular, personal Bible study and
prayer. Suppose we earnestly seek to know the mind of Jesus and
obediently follow where He leads. What do we find then? Some
answer that we discover dull monotony or at best a list of rules to
dully follow. This is generally said by those who have never taken
on Christ's yoke. Those who have followed Him find something
different. They find adventure, which I was speaking about at the

start of this chapter. They find freedom from self (even a freedom from rules in one sense), which is an amazing form of liberty.

It was the discovery of this freedom that led Elisabeth Elliot to write *The Liberty of Obedience.*³ She maintains that it is only in setting out to obey Christ completely that we find true freedom.

Jesus taught this too. He had been speaking of the source of His teachings, and many who listened had believed on Him. Their belief must have been rudimentary since no one, not even the disciples, understood that He was eventually going to the cross to die and thus provide redemption for His people. Nevertheless, this was real faith, and Jesus wanted to encourage it. He said, "If you hold to my teachings, you are really my disciples. Then you will know the truth, and the truth will set you free" (John 8:31-32).

This infuriated some of His listeners. They replied, "We are Abraham's descendants and have never been slaves of anyone. How can you say that we shall be set free?" (v. 33). This was ridiculous, of course. For years the Jews had been slaves in Egypt. During the period of the judges there were at least seven occasions when the nation came under the domination of foreigners. There was the seventy-year-long Babylonian captivity. Even as they talked to Jesus these people were watched by Roman soldiers and carried coins in their purses that proved Rome's rule over Palestine. It was this that made them so sensitive and provoked the retort "We . . . have never been slaves of anyone."

But how did Jesus respond? He did not show that they were deluded in their thoughts about political freedom, although He might have done that. Instead, He spoke of bondage to sin and showed that true freedom consists in escape from sin through obedience to Him. "I tell you the truth, everyone who sins is a slave to sin. . . . If the Son sets you free, you will be free indeed" (vv. 34, 36).

Freedom comes only as we determine to follow Jesus.

That freedom is the greatest freedom of all.

3. Elisabeth Elliot, *The Liberty of Obedience* (Nashville: Abingdon, 1981).

5

The Path of Service

You call me "Teacher" and "Lord," and rightly so, for that is what I am. Now that I, your Lord and Teacher, have washed your feet, you also should wash one another's feet. I have set you an example that you should do as I have done for you. I tell you the truth, no servant is greater than his master, nor is a messenger greater than the one who sent him. Now that you know these things, you will be blessed if you do them.

— John 13:13-17

Following the Lord Jesus Christ is an individual matter, but it is not individualistic.

When we say that discipleship is an individual matter we are saying that it is something that the individual himself must do. No one else can follow Jesus for you. Your wife cannot be your proxy. Your children cannot read the Bible for you, pray for you, obey the Lord for you. You must do these things yourself; and if you do not do them, you are not a true disciple. Individualism is something different. The dictionary defines individualism as "any doctrine or practice based on the assumption that the individual and not society is the paramount consideration or end." Christianity is not individualistic because it is never merely the individual but also all other persons who are in view.

The Lord indicated this when He responded to the question about the first commandment. He said that the first commandment is found in Deuteronomy 6:5, "Love the Lord your God with

all your heart and with all your soul and with all your strength."
But having spoken of the individual's relationship to God, Jesus
immediately went on to speak of the individual's relationship to
all other people, citing Leviticus 19:18: "And the second is like it:
'Love your neighbor as yourself.' All the Law and the Prophets
hang on these two commandments" (Matthew 22:39-40).

Love on Its Knees

What should our relationship to other persons be? Jesus said
that we are to love them, but how is that love shown? Do we show
love by some form of benevolent rule in the same way that a king
might be said to love his people? Do we love them the way a performer might be said to love his audience — or the way an audience might be said to love the performer? Christ's answer was that
we are to love others by serving them.

Jesus demonstrated what He had in mind. John tells us that at
the Last Supper, which Jesus observed with His disciples before
His arrest and crucifixion, the Master got up from the table, laid
His clothes aside, and then wrapping a towel around His waist,
poured water into a basin, got down on His knees, and began to
wash His disciples' feet, drying them with the towel that was
wrapped around Him.

An action like that was so unheard of that the outspoken Peter
objected, "Lord, are you going to wash my feet?" Jesus said, "You
do not realize now what I am doing, but later you will understand."

That was not enough for Peter, and he obviously thought he
understood well enough to rebuke the Lord, as he had before on
an earlier occasion ("Never, Lord! . . . This shall never happen to
you!" Matthew 16:22). Peter declared emphatically, "No, . . . you
shall never wash my feet." However, when Jesus explained that
unless He washed him Peter could have no part with Jesus, Peter
reversed himself, saying, "Then, Lord, . . . not just my feet but my
hands and my head as well!" He was still trying to tell Jesus how to
do things.

Jesus explained that He only needed to wash Peter's feet, the
very thing He had set out to do. Then He continued the foot
washing, rose, put His normal clothes back on, and returned to
His place. "Do you understand what I have done for you?" He
asked.

They obviously did not.

He continued, "You call me 'Teacher' and 'Lord,' and rightly so, for that is what I am. Now that I, your Lord and Teacher, have washed your feet, you also should wash one another's feet. I have set you an example that you should do as I have done for you. I tell you the truth, no servant is greater than his master, nor is a messenger greater than the one who sent him. Now that you know these things, you will be blessed if you do them" (John 13:13-17; cf. vv. 1-17).

According to that explanation, following Christ means serving others in accordance with His own example.

A PARABLE

His example was not just this one act of foot washing but rather His entire earthly ministry, of which the foot washing was a parable. Several chapters ago, when we were considering the meaning of self-denial, I compared the description of Jesus in Philippians 2:5-11 with the analysis of Satan recorded in Isaiah 14:12-14. Satan said, "I will go up. I will become like God. I will push God from His place." Jesus said, "I will go down. I will become like man. I will die to save him." This is one of the greatest, if not *the* greatest, contrasts of life — the contrast between Satan's way, which is also the way of the world, and God's way, embodied in Jesus Christ. This is precisely what we have in the incident of the foot washing. It is an illustration of the attitude that causes a person to serve others if he or she is a follower of Christ. It is stepping down for others' benefit.

Ray C. Stedman, pastor of the Peninsula Bible Church of Palo Alto, California, sees Christ's action as a parable of His entire ministry, comparing the verses from Philippians that I have just mentioned with what Jesus did for His disciples. John tells us that Jesus *got up* from supper. This had already been done in a far greater way when He rose from His throne of glory in preparation for His coming into the world. Second, He *took off* His outer clothing. Philippians says that when He came into the world He laid aside the glory that was naturally His, divesting Himself of the outward manifestations of His Godhead, and appeared as a true man so He would not blind us with His celestial glory. Next, He *wrapped a towel* around His waist. This was the uniform of a servant, a role which, Paul says, He took upon Himself. Finally, He *poured water* into a basin and began to wash the disciples' feet. In a few hours He was to pour out His blood for the washing away of human sin by the atonement.

The end of the parable comes after the foot washing, in verse 12. There we are told, "When he had finished washing their feet, he put on his clothes and returned to his place." In the same way, after His death and resurrection Jesus ascended to heaven and was seated again at the Father's right hand. Hebrews says, "After he had provided purification for sins, he sat down at the right hand of the Majesty in heaven" (Hebrews 1:3b).

Stedman concludes, "There can be little doubt that here Jesus was deliberately working out a parable for the instruction of his disciples. He was dramatizing for them the character of his ministry. He was showing them by this means what he had come into the world to do, and what he would send them out to do."[1]

When we see this parallel we see that Jesus was not instituting a new sacrament to be known as the sacrament of foot washing, though some have supposed this. He was talking about the need for those who would follow Him to take a servant role. He was saying, "I have been a servant to you. Everything I have done has been to serve you. Since I am your Teacher and Master, and yet have done this, you also should play a servant role with one another."

How to Serve Others

We must be practical at this point. Jesus served us by leaving heaven, taking on a true human nature, teaching, and then dying on the cross for our sin. We cannot do that. So we must ask, "How can *we* serve others? In what way must we demonstrate the servant nature of our Master?" I suggest the following.

1. *We must listen to others.* In *Life Together* Dietrich Bonhoeffer calls this the first part of genuine Christian service.

> The first service that one owes to others in the fellowship consists in listening to them. Just as love to God begins with listening to his word, so the beginning of love for the brethren is learning to listen to them. It is God's love for us that he not only gives us his word but also lends us his ear. So it is his work that we do for our brother when we learn to listen to him. Christians, especially ministers, so often think they must always contribute something when they are in the company of others, that this is the one service they have to render. They forget that

1. Ray C. Stedman, *Secrets of the Spirit* (Old Tappan, N.J.: Revell, 1975), p. 13.

listening can be a greater service than speaking.[2]

The reason that listening is so important is not always that people have a great deal to say but rather that they are desperate to have someone listen to them. Our world is characterized by a great cacophony of voices. People are shouting at us everywhere. They are shouting in commercials, in books and magazines, in signs by the roadside, at home, at work, at play. Everywhere we go someone is trying to get some message across to us. No one is listening to what we have to say. Everyone is too busy talking.

For many people life is like picking up a telephone, dialing a number, and getting a recording. We want to say, "Stop playing that thing, and listen to me." But, of course, no one is even listening to our complaint.

So we have the unique phenomenon in our day of people paying other people to listen to them, which is what the psychiatric, psychologic, and counseling professions are all about. Counseling is a billion-dollar business. But it is not that counselors actually advise or guide people in the vast majority of cases. Basically all they do is listen. They are paid to do what people in an earlier day did voluntarily.

Christians should be the greatest listeners this world has ever had. But unfortunately, they too are often talking instead of listening. Or even if we are listening, we are often listening only partially or impatiently, as we wait for the person to stop so we can get on with telling him what he should do to get right with God or get his life in order. Is that not true? Think of conversations you have had recently and ask yourself if your mind was not wandering as the other person spoke, if you were not hoping he or she would make it short, if you were not anxiously restless until you got your turn to speak. Ask yourself if your conversations with others are not mostly your sounding off about what interests you rather than really hearing the other person and responding directly to what he or she has to say.

If you are doing this, you should know that it is not only the other person who is harmed. You are harmed too, for, as Bonhoeffer astutely points out, "He who can no longer listen to his brother will soon be no longer listening to God either; he will be doing nothing but prattle in the presence of God too. This is the

2. Dietrich Bonhoeffer, Life Together, trans. John W. Doberstein (New York: Harper & Row, 1954), p. 97.

beginning of the death of the spiritual life, and in the end there is nothing left but spiritual chatter and clerical condescension arrayed in pious words."[3]

It is significant in regard to this part of Christian service that one of the tasks God has given His people is hearing one another's confessions (James 5:16). To hear a confession is something almost never practiced today — at least in the Protestant church. Protestants probably justify this as a rejection of what we regard as a Catholic error, that is, the saying of confession to a priest and the receiving of absolution by him in Christ's name. We are probably right in identifying the erroneous aspects of this practice. But is that really the reason we fail to hear confessions? Is it not rather that we are too busy talking to listen to what our fellow believer has to tell us? Is the other person not defrauded and harmed by our neglect? God listens to us and forgives us through the words of Scripture. We should listen to others, as God listens to us, so that we may speak the consoling words of God to them.

2. *We must help one another.* The desperation people have in needing to talk to someone is not always merely their desire to be heard, though that is important in itself. It is also often the case that they need help. Their speech is really a cry for assistance. If we stop to listen to people, we will find that their needs come rushing to the surface, and we have infinitely more to do than merely wash their feet. There will be people to feed, thirsty ones to whom to give a drink, naked people to clothe, lonely people to visit, sick and dying persons to care for, and so on for a host of other needs and obligations.

The problem is that helping people is seldom convenient. We have our own schedules and our own hours, and days are full. This is perhaps a bit truer of our time than earlier times due to the frantic pace of modern life, but our situation is not fundamentally different from what people of earlier days experienced. It is always inconvenient to help others. It was inconvenient for the Samaritan in Jesus' parable who helped the poor man who had fallen prey to thieves. He had his own journey. He too was on the way to Jericho. He too had business or family obligations. He interrupted these. He stopped his journey, attended to the wounded man, deviated from his itinerary in order to take the victim to an inn, spent the night, paid for his care, and then planned to return the

3. Ibid., p. 98.

same way after his own business was settled. This is what service means. It means putting others' well-being ahead of our own.

Bonhoeffer writes,

> It is a strange fact that Christians and even ministers frequently consider their work so important and urgent that they will allow nothing to disturb them. They think they are doing God a service in this, but actually they are distaining God's "crooked yet straight path" (Gottfried Arnold). They do not want a life that is crossed and balked. But it is part of the discipline of humility that we must not spare our hand where it can perform a service and that we do not assume that our schedule is our own to manage, but allow it to be arranged by God.[4]

3. *We must give to others.* The world says, "What's mine is mine, and what's yours is mine, if I can get it." The Christian says, "I have nothing but what I have first received from God, and therefore I am only a steward of my possessions. What's mine is yours, if you have need of it."

In the history of the church there have been Christians who have taken giving to others to the extreme of selling all they have had and distributing it to the poor or giving it to the church for its administration. At one point the Christians in Jerusalem did this (Acts 2:44-45). This is a form of Christian living that God may call some to at one time or another. But it is clear that this cannot be the whole of Christian obligation; for if all Christians in every place and at all times sold their goods and lived a common life in near-poverty conditions, no one would have anything to give to others again. To give to others does not mean that we must give everything or even that we should stop making money through honorable work. On the contrary, for some of us it could mean trying to make more so we will have more to give. It means that we must be generous with what we have, not counting it our own but rather that which God has given to us for others' benefits.

Then too, we must not forget that the best giving is often giving ourselves. When Paul wrote to the Corinthians about financial matters he commended the Macedonian churches for their rich generosity, explaining, "And they did not do as we expected, but they gave themselves first to the Lord and then to us in keeping with God's will" (2 Corinthians 8:5). Clearly, the Macedonians were able to be generous with their money because they had first

4. Ibid., p. 99.

been generous with themselves. Having given themselves to God and others, their material goods followed naturally.

4. *We must bear one another's burdens.* The Bible is able to express the whole work of Christ for us as bearing our burdens, "Surely he hath borne our griefs, and carried our sorrows" (Isaiah 53:4, KJV). So it is not surprising that it can describe the whole of the Christian life as bearing the cross and admonish us to "carry each other's burdens," saying, "and in this way you will fulfill the law of Christ" (Galatians 6:2).

Small groups are particularly important if we are to do that effectively. For how are we to carry others' burdens if we do not know what they are? How are we to learn about them unless we have a context in which Christians can confide in one another honestly? There are many problems at this point, one of which is our natural reluctance to let our hair down and confess what is bothering us. If we have problems with our schoolwork or our children, we hesitate to say so because admitting to what may be a failure leaves us vulnerable. We worry about what others think. Again, if we are having difficulties with husband or wife, we are afraid to admit it. We keep it in, and the problems build to the point where they sometimes prove unsolvable. How are Christians to share their burdens in such areas? The easiest way is through building acceptance in a small-group setting.

There is another advantage of the small group. Often people come into our orbit who have tremendous problems. They need so much physical help or psychological and emotional rebuilding that one person, or even one family, simply cannot meet the need — even with the best of will and intentions. In a small group the task is distributed, and the one being helped can get back on his or her feet without developing an unbalanced and unhealthy dependence on one person.

In Dietrich Bonhoeffer's study of these themes there is a useful development of "bearing" in the area of another person's freedom and sins. The freedom of the other is often a burden, because it collides with our own autonomy. Anyone who has ever tried to help another needy person knows what this means, because one of the things that makes helping another so difficult is that the person generally does not contribute to the process and in fact usually fights against it at our expense. He refuses to fall in step with us. So we find ourselves having to shoulder that burden as well.

In a previous chapter we talked about denying oneself and taking up our cross. There is probably no area of the Christian life where this is more necessary or more difficult. To bear another's burdens, particularly those of an extremely disoriented and needy person, means involvement with him or her at our own cost and inconvenience, which means we will only be able to bear it by a genuine crucifixion of ourselves.

What about sin in the other person? It is not just freedom that inconveniences. Sin divides. It divides the individual from God, but it also divides the individual from all other individuals — in this case ourselves. In trying to bear the other's burdens we are often sinned against, and a barrier comes up. The only way we can deal with this is by the recognition that it was "while we were still sinners, Christ died for us" (Romans 5:8). Jesus did not wait for us to get better or even repent of our sin. He died for us while we were still rebellious. In the same way, we are to die to self for others, knowing that it is by the example of such selfless love that God generally wins sinners to Himself.

Bonhoeffer writes, "Since every sin of every member burdens and indicts the whole community, the congregation rejoices, in the midst of all the pain and the burden the brother's sin inflicts, that it has the privilege of bearing and forgiving."[5]

5. *We must speak God's truth to the other person.* When I began this listing of what it means to serve others I said that Christians tend to talk without listening, assuming that they already know what is about to be said and that they already have the answer to it. I stressed that service begins with real listening. That is true; it is an important first requirement. But having said that, we need to realize that there is also a time to speak and that Christians are distinguished from others at this point by having something genuinely helpful to say — because they can speak God's words as they have heard them in Scripture. This gives us service far ahead of secular psychologists and counselors. They listen — often better than we do. They offer wise advice or counsel. But the help of a purely secular counselor stops there. The Christian, once he has heard and understood, can go on to share the cure for the problem or the hope for the despair given by God in the Bible.

Many persons have a natural reluctance to instruct another person, particularly another believer. They are conscious, as we should all be, that they are often confused themselves. But fear of

5. Ibid., p. 103.

our own proneness to failure should not keep us from saying what is necessary at the proper time. The Christians at Rome had not had benefit of apostolic instruction when Paul wrote to them, but he said, "I myself am convinced, my brothers, that you yourselves are full of goodness, complete in knowledge and competent to instruct one another" (Romans 15:14).

Bonhoeffer is right on this point:

> Where Christians live together the time must inevitably come when in some crisis one person will have to declare God's word and will to another. It is inconceivable that the things that are of utmost importance to each individual should not be spoken by one to another. It is unchristian to consciously deprive another of the one decisive service we can render to him. If we cannot bring ourselves to utter it, we shall have to ask ourselves whether we are not still seeing our brother garbed in his human dignity which we are afraid to touch, and thus forgetting the most important thing, that he, too, no matter how old or highly placed or distinguished he may be, is still a man like us, a sinner in crying need of God's grace. He has the same great necessities that we have, and needs help, encouragement and forgiveness as we do.[6]

At times we must speak words that sound harsh to the one who has to hear them. It is difficult to speak such words. More often, it is our privilege to speak words of comfort that the Bible contains. We may have to speak of sin. But we can always also speak of God's grace and forgiveness. We can tell our brother, "If we confess our sins, he is faithful and just and will forgive us our sins and purify us from all unrighteousness" (1 John 1:9). We can assure him that, if he has confessed his sin, God has already forgiven it for Jesus' sake.

6. *We must restore one another.* Speaking the truth in love, which includes the exposure of sin and the pronouncement of forgiveness for the one who repents of it and turns to Christ, has as its object the complete restoration of the other person. In aiding in this we perform what is perhaps our greatest form of service.

Here we get closest to what Christ's example of foot washing was all about. In His explanation of His actions to Peter we learn that Jesus chiefly had in mind cleansing from the defilement of sin

6. Ibid., p. 105.

followed by the restoration of the one sinning. When Jesus told Peter, "A person who has had a bath needs only to wash his feet; his whole body is clean. And you are clean, though not every one of you," it was evident that He was not thinking about physical dirt but about sin and the way to be cleansed from it through justification and a subsequent growth in grace. He was telling Peter that He was a justified person and therefore needed only to be cleansed from the contaminating effects of sin and not from sin's penalty.

The image is of an Oriental who would bathe completely before going to another person's home for dinner. On the way, because he would be shod in sandals and because the streets were dirty, his feet would become contaminated. When he arrived at his friend's home his feet would need to be washed but not his whole body. In a parallel way, those who are Christ's are justified men and women, but they do need constant cleansing from their repeated defilement by sin in order that the fellowship they have with the Father and Son might not be broken. It was Jesus' washing of His disciples' feet, not their heads or entire bodies, that Jesus commended to us by His example. If we carry this out in spiritual terms, as we must, we must seek to restore others from sin's defilement. We must do as Paul admonished the Galatians, "Brothers, if someone is caught in a sin, you who are spiritual should restore him gently. But watch yourself, or you also may be tempted" (Galatians 6:1).

How do we seek to restore a brother who has fallen into some sin? How do we seek to wash the feet of such a one? We are to take the Word of God and then gently, ever so gently, apply it to him, desiring that he might respond to it by the grace of God.

Notice that I said "gently." In his commentary on these verses Harry A. Ironside points out that if we are going to wash another's feet, we ought to be careful of the temperature of the water. You would not go to anyone and say, "Here, put your feet into this bucket of scalding water." Nor would you ask him to place his feet in a bucket of ice water. It is just as bad to be too hot in approaching another person as it is to be too cold and formal. Stedman points out that in trying to cleanse others some Christians attempt to do without water at all. They try to dry-clean feet. They scrape them free of dirt and unfortunately sometimes take the skin with it.[7] Instead of this, we are to approach the other in meekness and great love, realizing that we are capable of the same sin ourselves.

The Path to Happiness

The last lines of our text deserve special attention, for in them Jesus speaks of being blessed, or happy, and gives the secret for such happiness: "Now that you know these things, you will be blessed if you do them" (v. 17). Most people want to be happy, and they suppose, as sinful men and women do, that the way to be happy is to be served by other people — to have them meet our needs. Jesus says the opposite. He says that happiness comes in serving others.

Will you serve others? Will you *do* what Jesus tells you to do? For most Christians the problem is at this point. They know Christ's teaching to the extent that most of what I have written in this chapter is not fundamentally new for them. They know they should follow the Lord in self-denying service to other people. They know they should listen to, help, give to, support, instruct, and restore others. That is Jesus' way. They even know that they will be blessed by Jesus if they do. Yet although they know these things, they do not do them but rather continue to live for self, which is the world's way.

A number of years ago, shortly after a very severe drop in the stock market, I was talking to a man who had approximately half a million dollars invested. "Did the drop affect you greatly?" I asked him.

"It certainly did," he told me.

"Did you have any idea that the market might be going down?" I asked.

"That's the funny thing," he replied. "About two months before the market tumbled, when the Dow Jones was still over one thousand, some of us who invested together were meeting. I remember saying that the market simply could not continue as it was. I said it would have to go back down. Surprisingly, everyone agreed. When I said that we ought to sell now, they agreed to that too. But, you know, nobody did it. None of us sold. So when the bottom dropped out, all of us were left with large losses."

Success in the Christian life does not come from mere knowledge alone, though knowledge is important. It comes from doing what we know we should do. To follow Jesus means serving others. This path leads to blessing. We will be happy only if we walk in it.

7. Stedman, p. 20.

6

The Path of Humility

You know that the rulers of the Gentiles lord it over them, and their high officials exercise authority over them. Not so with you. Instead, whoever wants to become great among you must be your servant, and whoever wants to be first must be your slave — just as the Son of Man did not come to be served, but to serve, and to give his life as a ransom for many.

— Matthew 20:25-28

Years ago a woman who attended one of my Bible classes gave me a book that she earnestly wanted me to read. It was entitled *Beyond Humiliation.* I did not read it. I was conscious of my own lack of humility and thought that reading a book going "beyond" humility was the last thing I needed. It would be the height of pride to think of going beyond something I had not even begun to attain.

By contrast I think of Brother Lawrence, whose collected conversations and letters are entitled *The Practice of the Presence of God.* Lawrence lived in the seventeenth century. He was born Nicholas Herman in French Lorraine, served as a soldier, and then was converted through seeing a tree in winter, stripped of its leaves, and reflecting on the fact that within a short time its leaves would be renewed through the love and power of God. His conversion led him to enter the monastery of the barefooted Carmelites at Paris in 1666. In the monastery Lawrence, as he was then called, was assigned to the kitchen, where he had charge of utensils. At first he abhorred the work. But he set himself to walk in God's presence so that he could worship God and serve others in the most humble circumstances. In time Brother Lawrence came to worship God more in the kitchen than in the cathedral, praying, "Lord of all pots and pans and things, . . . make me a saint by getting meals and washing up the plates." He died at eighty years of age, full of love and honored by all who knew him. His meditations on the Christian life, recorded largely by others, are a classic.

A Difficult School

How little we know of humility, even after many years of Christian life. Yet how essential humility is to true discipleship! In previous chapters I pointed out that discipleship means following Jesus Christ and that it is essential for all who would be saved by Him. I referred to Christ's *obedience* in leaving heaven in order to become like us and die for our salvation. But I need to note that it was not only the path of obedience that Jesus' incarnation marked out. He modeled *humiliation* as well. Philippians 2:8, which is the chief statement in this area, says, "And being found in appearance as a man, he *humbled* himself and became obedient to death — even death on a cross!" (my emphasis). Obedience and humility are both virtues in which believers must imitate Christ — the need for obedience is mentioned in verse 12, humility in verse 3. It is for the sake of learning humility that this was written.

But it is a difficult school, which is the point I am making. Obedience is hard, too, though there are times when we believe we can almost handle it. Humility takes us back to the need to die to self and take up our cross and is the hardest thing of all.

It was hard even for the disciples, who had been taught by Christ and had continued in His school for three years. In the last chapter I looked at the Lord's parable of Christian service — His washing of His disciples' feet. I pointed out areas in which we must serve other people. But what I did not talk about in that chapter was the reason the Lord was particularly led to this demonstration. The problem was that the disciples had been fighting over who should be greatest in the kingdom, which they supposed Jesus would soon bring. They were thinking of pomp and circumstance, not the cross. They assumed that Jesus was going to take over the throne of His father David, and they were jockeying to see who would stand closest to that throne, exercise the greatest influence, and receive the greatest honor in that day.

This had happened on several occasions. After the transfiguration, when the disciples who had remained behind had been approached by the father of a boy with an evil spirit and had been unable to drive the spirit out, the group fell to arguing. We are not told this, but the three who had been with Jesus on the mountain probably thought themselves superior to the nine who had remained behind and had failed in the matter of the exorcism. They had been arguing about who was greatest (Mark 9:34). Jesus instructed them, saying, "If anyone wants to be first, he must be the very last, and the servant of all" (v. 35).

Then Jesus used an illustration. He drew a little child into their midst and said, "Whoever welcomes one of these little children in my name welcomes me; and whoever welcomes me does not welcome me but the one who sent me" (v. 37; cf. Matthew 18:1-5; Luke 9:46-48).

We would think that the disciples would get the point, particularly since it had been reinforced for them visually. But in the very next chapters of Matthew and Mark, each of whom tells the story, we find the disciples actually turning children aside. They have been telling their mothers that Jesus is too important, too busy. But really they are thinking that *they* are too busy. Besides, any time spent by Jesus on the children would not be spent on them. Jesus was indignant with the disciples. He said, "Let the little children come to me, and do not hinder them, for the kingdom of God belongs to such as these. I tell you the truth, anyone who will not receive the kingdom of God like a little child will never enter it" (Mark 10:14-15; cf. Matthew 19:14; Luke 18:16-17).

This was an intensification of His earlier teaching. Earlier He had spoken of relative positions within His kingdom — the first would be last and the last first. Now He was teaching that without humility it was not possible even to enter the kingdom.

A third incident came before the triumphal entry. On this occasion the mother of James and John came asking if her sons could sit on the right and left sides of Jesus when He came in His kingdom. The other disciples heard about it and got angry with James and John. Jesus said, "You know that the rulers of the Gentiles lord it over them, and their high officials exercise authority over them. Not so with you. Instead, whoever wants to become great among you must be your servant, and whoever wants to be first must be your slave — just as the Son of Man did not come to be served, but to serve, and to give his life as a ransom for many"

(Matthew 20:25-28; cf. Mark 10:42-45).

We would think perhaps that now, after that episode and lecture, the disciples would have learned their lesson and that their desire for the chief place would be forgotten. But this was not so. Apparently the conflict intensified and continued even into the upper room. For if Luke is giving us a chronological account of this evening, we learn that even after the institution of the Lord's Supper "a dispute arose among them as to which of them was considered to be greatest" (Luke 22:24). It was at this point perhaps that the Lord divested Himself of His clothing and performed the foot washing. If we can learn from the disciples, we should learn that the desire to be foremost is so great in us that we can be maneuvering for prominence even as we come to the Communion service.

So when Jesus washed His disciples' feet, He was not speaking only about service, though that is the way in which we studied John 13 in the last chapter. He was also speaking about humility, saying that humility is the prerequisite for service. It is only when we become like a little child — no, even more, a slave — that we can really follow Jesus and help others.

Also, it is only when we become like little children that we can learn from Jesus, learning among other things what humility is and how it must function. Otherwise we are like the disciples. We are so caught up with thoughts of our own importance that we do not even hear Christ speaking.

Four Burdens Rolled Away

One of the greatest books on the Christian life that I have read is A. W. Tozer's The Pursuit of God. He deals with humility in this book and says that learning humility from Jesus delivers us from four crushing burdens.

1. The burden of pride. Humility is the opposite of pride. So to the extent that we learn meekness in Christ's school, so far are we delivered from the destructive weight of self-love, pride, and arrogance. The burden of pride is a heavy one. In his study Tozer asks us to consider how much trouble has come into our own lives because of our prideful reaction to someone who has given us offense.

As long as you set yourself up as a little god to which you must be loyal there will be those who will delight to offer affront to your idol. How then can you hope to have inward peace? The heart's fierce effort to protect itself from every slight, to shield its touchy honor from the bad opinion of friend and enemy, will never let the mind have rest. Continue this fight through the years and the burden will become intolerable. Yet the sons of earth are carrying this burden continually, challenging every word spoken against them, cringing under every criticism, smarting under each fancied slight, tossing sleepless if another is preferred before them.[1]

We think of Moses, who is praised in the Bible as "a very humble man, more humble than anyone else on the face of the earth" (Numbers 12:3). He is praised for this spirit in a story in which he experienced the worst of personal attacks — not from a distant enemy, but from Miriam and Aaron, his sister and brother.

Forty years before this time, when Moses had fled Egypt and had lived in Midian, he had married Zipporah, the daughter of a priest named Reuel. Zipporah was of the same racial stock as the Israelites, and she had borne children to Moses. However, Zipporah had died by the time this later story takes place, and Moses was marrying another wife. His new wife was a Cushite, the name given to the inhabitants of ancient Ethiopia, and the point of the story lies in the fact that she was therefore of different racial stock from the Jews. Probably she was black. We can not be entirely sure of this, but it is likely since the Cushites were generally regarded as black and because of the particular details of the later punishment of Miriam, who objected to the marriage. The text says, "Miriam and Aaron began to talk against Moses because of his Cushite wife, for he had married a Cushite. 'Has the Lord spoken only through Moses?' they asked. 'Hasn't he also spoken through us?' " (vv. 1-2).

The Bible tells us that God heard the words of Miriam and Aaron and at once called them to stand before the Tent of Meeting. He said,

> When a prophet of the Lord is among you,
>   I reveal myself to him in visions,
>   I speak to him in dreams.
> But this is not true of my servant Moses;

1. A. W. Tozer, *The Pursuit of God* (Harrisburg, Pa.: Christian Publications, 1948), p. 112.

> he is faithful in all my house.
> With him I speak face to face,
> clearly and not in riddles;
> he sees the form of the Lord.
> Why then were you not afraid
> to speak against my servant Moses?
>   (Numbers 12:6-8)

The story continues by saying that the anger of the Lord burned against them and that, when the cloud lifted from the Tent of Meeting, "there stood Miriam — leprous" (v. 10). It is this fact that makes me think Moses' new wife was black. By the form of Miriam's punishment it was as though God were saying, "You're brown. This girl is black, and you think white is better. All right, have more of it." So she became a leper, and God used the incident to teach that there was to be no racial prejudice in Israel.

At the end of the story we find Moses praying for his sister, who was later healed. This is the chief point: namely, the gentle conduct of Moses throughout the attack. What was his deportment? Did he resent his sister's accusations? Did he retaliate? Did he fight back? He did none of these things, because he was walking in the path of humility and was therefore delivered from the burden of pride that makes us want to defend our own rights. Moses was humble because he had bowed down before God. Therefore, he was able to stand tall but humbly before men and women.

2. *The burden of pretense.* The second burden Tozer writes about is the burden of pretense — pretending to be something we are not and hiding what we are. The man who is moderately successful in business tries to look wildly successful. He is ashamed to be thought only a moderate achiever. A person of limited education pretends to be more highly educated than he or she is and fears to meet a thoroughly educated man. Even if well educated, the person fears to meet one who is better educated or to be in a position where the unfavorable comparison shows. A cultured person fears to be with those who are even more cultured. Tozer says, "Let no one smile this off. These burdens are real, and little by little they kill the victims of this evil and unnatural way of life."[2]

We pretend because we fear to be known as we really are. We do not want another person to think us ill-informed, gauche, un-

2. Ibid., p. 114.

sophisticated, or other such things. But the real problem is that we are sinners, and our real fear (although we do not often admit it, even to ourselves) is that someone will find out that we are corrupt and our hearts desperately wicked, as the prophet Jeremiah wrote (Jeremiah 17:9).

Jesus delivers us from pretense when we follow Him. He does it by bringing us before Himself, face to face with God before whom "all hearts are opened, all desires known." If our basic problem is sin and the desire to hide it from others, then the cure is to have sin dealt with by Christ and know that we are accepted by God on the basis of Jesus' atoning work, regardless of what we are or have done. Another way of saying this is that the cure for our fear is knowing that we are known already — deeply and exhaustively by God Himself and that He has loved us and receives us anyway. Humility begins by knowing that I am accepted by God. Therefore, since I can stand before God without the need to pretend, I can also stand before others. If I am accepted by God, I do not need to worry about what others may think of my performance.

3. *The burden of artificiality.* Artificiality is a problem closely linked to pretense, as Tozer indicates. But it is a step beyond it — a step in the wrong direction. It involves a fear of relaxing and an enforced affectation. It is what we mean when we say that a person always seems to be "playing a role." It can be amusing at times, but it wears thin, and we come away feeling that we really do not know the person. "I wish he (or she) would just relax and be himself," we say.

Artificiality falls away at the cross of Christ. The cross is so real, so brutally authentic, that standing before it is like standing before a bright light that probes into every recess of our being. Before the cross we have the experience of the children in the *Chronicles of Narnia* whenever they were with Aslan. Before him any dishonest word, any self-serving statement, tended to dry up — not so much because they feared he would punish them for deceit, but because evil simply could not stand before one who was both all-powerful and completely good. The one who is following Jesus will have precisely this experience. If we walk with Christ, we will grow in humility. If we are not walking in humility, if pride, pretense, and artificiality are not falling away in our lives, we are not living for Christ. If we are as proud as we were before our alleged "conversion," we are not His.

4. *The burden of self-struggle.* A fourth burden we are delivered from if we walk in humility is struggle, struggle somehow to "make it" or "gain recognition" in this world. You will understand, I am sure, that I am not encouraging a lazy spirit or an indifferent attitude in serving Christ. In His service there is always need for hard work, diligence, willingness to suffer, and great perseverance. But that is a different thing from that kind of struggle for self-advancement that flows from pride. The apostle Paul said, "Forgetting what is behind and straining toward what is ahead, I press on toward the goal to win the prize for which God has called me heavenward in Christ Jesus" (Philippians 3:13-14). Yet in the same letter he wrote, "I have learned to be content whatever the circumstances" (Philippians 4:11).

Jeremiah Burroughs was a seventeenth-century Puritan who reflected on the strange lack of contentment he saw about him in the church. In response he wrote *The Rare Jewel of Christian Contentment.* He explained a lack of contentment as failure to see ourselves as we truly are, which means that lack of contentment flows from pride. His cure was to be steeped in the teaching of Christ, knowing: (1) that in ourselves we are nothing; (2) that we deserve nothing; (3) that we can do nothing; (4) that we are worse than nothing, since sin pits us against the good; (5) that if we perish, it will be no loss; and (6) that our chief wisdom consists in the denial of self and the taking up of our cross in Christ's service. Burroughs wrote,

> There was never any man or woman so contented as a self-denying man or woman. No one ever denied himself as much as Jesus Christ did: he gave his cheeks to the smiters, he opened not his mouth, he was as a lamb when he was led to the slaughter, he made no noise in the street. He denied himself above all, and was willing to empty himself, and so he was the most contented that ever any was in the world. The nearer we come to learning to deny ourselves as Christ did, the more contented shall we be.[3]

Burroughs was right in exalting contentment as an important Christian virtue. So long as we are proud we shall judge that our status and rewards in life are less than we deserve, and we will be constantly striving to grasp what we consider our due. We will be

---

3. Jeremiah Burroughs, *The Rare Jewel of Christian Contentment* (Carlisle, Pa.: Banner of Truth Trust, 1964), pp. 89-90. Original edition 1648.

unhappy! If we bow before Christ, we will marvel at how greatly He has blessed us, whatever we have, and we will rest in that. Paul said, "I have learned the secret of being content in any and every situation, whether well fed or hungry, whether living in plenty or in want. I can do everything through him who gives me strength" (Philippians 4:12-13).

Begin with God

So I say again: If we are to learn humility (which we must do, if we are walking in the path marked out for us by Christ), we must begin with God and see everything in relation to Him, rather than in relation to ourselves. That is, we must acknowledge and embrace the fact that this is a God-centered and not a man-centered universe.

I return to the disciples, the point from which this chapter started out. In the closing days of Christ's earthly life, as He was attempting to prepare them for His departure and instruct them in what they would need to know to function as His disciples after He was gone, they were arguing about who should be greatest. They were thinking of themselves rather than about Him. He was about to make that sacrifice upon which the meaning of all reality centers. The uplifted cross was to be the focal point of history. But the disciples? They were not thinking of that. They were thinking about Christ's earthly kingdom, and they were jockeying for the most prominent places in it. They were doing everything I have described. They were prideful, pretending to be what they were not, guarding their ground and struggling to emerge either at Christ's right hand or His left. They were trapped by these drives, so much so that they missed what Christ was saying and almost missed the greatest event of all. Yet they did not miss it in the end, because Christ prayed for them and sent His Holy Spirit to change them and awaken them to the truth.

It is beautiful to see. The disciples were all guilty of this fighting spirit, according to the gospel accounts. But among the many guilty, James and John stand out as most guilty because of their compliance in the efforts of their mother to get them the first places. Yet think what happened. At one time Jesus called them "Sons of Thunder," no doubt because of their arrogant, boisterous attitudes (Mark 3:17). On another occasion they wanted to call down fire from heaven to destroy a village of the Samaritans that did not receive them (Luke 9:54). But they changed when they finally got their minds off themselves and onto Jesus.

We are not told much about James, but he must have changed. We never hear of his struggling for prominence after the crucifixion and resurrection of the Lord, and he eventually died for Jesus, executed by King Herod (Acts 12:1-2). John lived to be a venerable old man, known as the "apostle of love." He was living humility when he said, "This is how we know what love is: Jesus Christ laid down his life for us. And we ought to lay down our lives for our brothers" (1 John 3:16).

If Jesus can turn a "son of thunder" into an "apostle of love," He can conquer pride in us and teach us humility.

He needs to, if we are truly to be His disciples.

7

Traveling Light

Take nothing for the journey except a staff — no bread, no bag, no money in your belts. Wear sandals but not an extra tunic. Whenever you enter a house, stay there until you leave that town. And if any place will not welcome you or listen to you, shake the dust off your feet when you leave, as a testimony against them.

— Mark 6:8-11

I received a letter from a couple going to the mission field for the first time. It listed their financial requirements: so much for support, medical expenses, insurance, pension, the cost of operating an automobile, travel to and from the field, overhead for the home office, and so on. I was not disturbed by the letter. I was actually quite sympathetic. I knew that the requests were reasonable. Still I could not help contrasting their letter with the Lord's commands to the disciples when they set out on their first missionary journey. He told them to go without possessions: "Take nothing for the journey except a staff — no bread, no bag, no money in your belts. Wear sandals but not an extra tunic. Whenever you enter a house, stay there until you leave that town. And if any place will not welcome you or listen to you, shake the dust off your feet when you leave, as a testimony against them" (Mark 6:8-11).

This list of instructions highlights the uneasy alliance most Christians have with their possessions. We admire Saint Francis of Assisi who stripped himself of everything and went off singing into the forest. But we do not follow his example. On the contrary, we spend most of our lives making money; and if we are honest, we admit that for the most part we do not make money in order to have more to help others. We make it to spend on ourselves.

We are disturbed by Christ's saying "Any of you who does not give up everything he has cannot be my disciple" (Luke 14:33).

WEALTH AND POVERTY

Part of the problem comes from what seems, on the surface, to be contradictory statements in Scripture. In the text first quoted, when Jesus sends His disciples off on their journey, He tells them, "Take nothing." But at the Last Supper He referred to that earlier incident, saying, "When I sent you without purse, bag or sandals, did you lack anything?" and when they answered no, He continued, "But now if you have a purse, take it, and also a bag; and if you don't have a sword, sell your cloak and buy one" (Luke 22:35-36).

When the rich young ruler approached Jesus, asking, "Good teacher, what must I do to inherit eternal life?" Jesus answered, "Do not murder, do not commit adultery, do not steal, do not give false testimony, do not defraud, honor your father and mother." The young man said he had kept all those commandments since he was a boy. Jesus responded, "One thing you lack. . . . Go, sell everything you have and give to the poor, and you will have treasure in heaven. Then come, follow me" (Mark 10:17-21). This clearly indicated that the young man's wealth was keeping him from salvation. In order to be saved it was necessary for him to sell his possessions and give all he had to the poor. But Jesus did not make this demand of Peter or James or John or countless others. He made it of a rich young man whose riches were *in his case* a barrier to salvation.

Even Ananias and Sapphira were not judged for failing to give up their possessions but for lying about what they did — pretending to have given all when actually they were keeping part. When Peter asked Ananias, "Didn't it [the land] belong to you before it was sold? And after it was sold, wasn't the money at your disposal?" (Acts 5:4), he was actually establishing the right of private property.

Many psalms suggest that material blessing is the rightful expectation of the devout man.

You still the hunger of those you cherish;

their sons have plenty,
and they store up wealth for their children.
(Psalm 17:14)

Who, then, is the man that fears the Lord?
He will instruct him in the way chosen for him.
He will spend his days in prosperity.
(Psalm 25:12-13)

Blessed is the man who fears the Lord. . . .
Wealth and riches are in his house,
and his righteousness endures forever.
(Psalm 112:1-2)

Our barns will be filled
with every kind of provision.
Our sheep will increase by thousands,
by tens of thousands in our fields.
(Psalm 144:13)

On the other hand, the Bible is filled with warnings against riches. J. C. Ryle, the evangelical English bishop of an earlier generation, put it like this:

Is it for nothing that the Lord Jesus spoke the parable of the rich fool and blamed him because he was not "rich towards God" (Luke 12:21)? Is it for nothing that in the parable of the sower he mentions the "deceitfulness of riches" as one reason why the seed of the Word bears no fruit (Matt. 13:22)? Is it for nothing that he says, "Make to yourselves friends of the mammon of unrighteousness" (Luke 16:9)? Is it for nothing that he says, "When thou makest a dinner or a supper, call not thy friends, nor thy brethren, neither thy kinsmen, nor thy rich neighbors; lest they also bid thee again, and a recompense be made thee. But when thou makest a feast, call the poor, the maimed, the lame, the blind: and thou shalt be blessed; for they cannot recompense thee; for thou shalt be recompensed at the resurrection of the just" (Luke 14:12-14)? Is it for nothing that he says, "Sell that ye have and give alms; provide yourselves bags which wax not old, a treasure in the heavens that faileth not, where no thief approacheth, neither moth corrupteth" (Luke 12:33)? Is it for nothing that he says, "It is more blessed to give than to receive" (Acts 20:35)? Is it for nothing that he warns us against the example of the priest and Levite, who saw the wounded traveller, but passed by on the other side? Is it for nothing that

he praises the good Samaritan, who denied himself to show
kindness to a stranger (Luke 10:30 ff.)? Is it for nothing that St.
Paul classes covetousness with sins of the grossest description
and denounces it as idolatry (Col. 3:5)? And is there not a striking and painful difference between this language and the habits
and feeling of society about money?[1]

On the surface at least, some of these statements seem to con-
tradict each other. However, the more we study them, the more
we are convinced that the problem is not in the texts but in ourselves. It is in our attitude to riches. Our attitude keeps us from
handling wealth as God would have us handle it.

A. W. Tozer, in a chapter called "The Blessedness of Possessing
Nothing," points out that "before the Lord God made man upon
the earth he first prepared for him by creating a world of useful and
pleasant things for his sustenance and delight." But he adds cor-
rectly, "Sin has introduced complications and has made those very
gifts of God a potential source of ruin to the soul."[2]

A friend of mine puts it this way. He says that we all have desires and that there is nothing wrong with desires in themselves.
The problem is that we have infinite desires — we always want
more — and since only God is infinite, it follows that we can never be satisfied with anything but God. Augustine said, "Thou hast
made us for thyself, and our hearts are restless until they find their
rest in thee" (Confessions, I, 1, i). When we try to fill our lives
with things, we commit idolatry, misuse our possessions, harm
others, and condemn ourselves to frustration and eternal loss.

ALL GOOD GIFTS FROM GOD

Where should we go to get a proper perspective on riches?
Where can we learn to relate our possessions to our discipleship?
Negatively there is much to be said about things, but the place to
begin is not with a negative but with a positive: *All things come
from God.* God is the Creator. Therefore, possessions are to be received from Him with thanksgiving and are to be enjoyed fully as
He intended them to be enjoyed. James wrote, "Every good and
perfect gift is from above, coming down from the Father of the
heavenly lights, who does not change like shifting shadows"
(James 1:17).

---

1. J. C. Ryle, *Practical Religion* (Cambridge: James Clarke, 1959), p. 216.
2. A. W. Tozer, *The Pursuit of God* (Harrisburg, Pa.: Christian Publications, 1948), p. 21.

There is a false idea in some forms of Christianity that things somehow are evil and that the only way to live a truly spiritual life is to part with them. It may be true, of course, as in the case of the rich young man, that the only way a given individual can find salvation is by repudiating the wealth that keeps him from discipleship. But that is not because things in themselves are evil. That view was present in the ancient world but was repudiated by Christianity. That view was *dualism*. It said that there are two spheres of reality: the sphere of mind or spirit (which is good) and the sphere of things or matter (which is evil). By nature, men and women are amalgamations; they possess a mind (which relates them to God and draws them upward) and a body (which is evil and draws them downward). The only way to be saved is to escape from the body. In life this is done by living in the realm of the mind and denying physical pleasures.

In the Greek world dualism produced the distinct formulations of its great philosophers. In the Christian world dualism produced monasticism.

Christianity does not teach dualism. According to the Bible, all that we see and know was created by God and in its original form — that is, before the Fall and the distortions that came from it — was pronounced utterly good by Him. Our bodies are from God; they are good. Our minds are from God; they too are good. The fruit of the field is good. The fruit of our labor — seen in homes and buildings and manufactured goods and social services and writing and art — is good. God has given us fields, hills, mountains, seas, storms, sunrises, and sunsets all richly to enjoy.

But there is this to be said. First, it is God who has given these things. And because God is sovereign in His giving, as in everything else, it follows that He may (and, in fact, does) give some more than others and that this is also good and just. That is the Christian answer to egalitarianism, the idea that all people must be equal in riches and that, if they are not, it is the job of government or some other outside agency to redistribute them. This is not government's job. The government is established by God to promote and enforce justice (Romans 13:1-5). If one individual grows rich by extorting goods from others, by fraud or by actions that deny or destroy basic human values and rights, it is government's job to expose the evil, punish the injustice, and demand restitution. The government must not take what belongs to one individual (if it is lawfully acquired) and give it to another. That is itself an injustice. There is nothing in nature or Scripture to say that all persons must possess an equal share of this world's goods; and, in fact, it is evident that even God does not so distribute His good gifts. One servant will always have five talents, another two, and a third just one.

Second, because the things we possess are given to us by God it follows that we are accountable to Him for how we use them. This is what the parable of the talents is about. God distributes His gifts unequally — one servant has five talents, another two, a third one — but each is nevertheless equally responsible for the proper use of what he has been given. The man who is judged by Christ is judged, not because he had one talent rather than two or five, but because he did not properly use that one talent he had. So will we be, if we fail to use God's gifts properly.

A CHRISTIAN PERSPECTIVE

So I come back to my original question and ask again: What should a disciple's attitude to his possessions be? We have seen that he may have great possessions or few. He may be required to give up his possessions if he is to follow Christ, though this is not usually the case. But assuming that the disciple of Christ possesses some things, whether many or few, how should he regard them and what place should they have in his life? I suggest the following principles.

1. *Thanksgiving.* First Timothy 4:4 says, "Everything God created is good, and nothing is to be rejected if it is received with thanksgiving." A Christian perspective starts at this point.

God desires to give. In fact, God desires to give lavishly; He has already given lavishly; and there is a sense in which He will continue to give lavishly to His own people throughout eternity. It is true that at times God also takes away, but that is for the same reason that He more frequently gives, namely, because He loves us. If something is standing in the way of our spiritual growth or usefulness, God will remove it. But that aside, God's main relationship to us is that of an abundant giver. We cannot exist without His benevolence. God gives life and health, sun and rain, friends and families, opportunities to learn and serve and worship — indeed, all things. So our first proper response to this must be thanksgiving.

This implies two further things. First, *humility.* If all we have is from God, then we must be humble about it and not boast of our possessions as if we had somehow achieved them without God. Paul makes this point in 1 Corinthians 4:7. "What do you have that you did not receive? And if you did receive it, why do you boast as though you did not?" To boast is the opposite of being thankful.

Second, *contentment*. Elisabeth Elliot writes,

> Thanksgiving requires the recognition of the Source. It implies contentment with what is given, not complaint about what is not given. It excludes covetousness. The goodness and love of God choose the gifts, and we say thank you, acknowledging the Thought Behind as well as the thing itself. Covetousness involves suspicion about the goodness and love of God, and even his justice. He has not given me what he gave somebody else. He doesn't notice my need. He doesn't love me as much as he loves him. He isn't fair. Faith looks up with open hands. "You are giving me this, Lord? Thank you. It is good and acceptable and perfect."[3]

If we are not content, we are not thankful. The apostle Paul called "godliness with *contentment*" great gain (1 Timothy 6:6, my emphasis).

2. *Perspective.* The second important element in a disciple's attitude toward his possessions is perspective. Although it is true that all things are given to us by God and are grounds for thanksgiving, material possessions are nevertheless not the only things God gives or even the most important things. If we fail to see this, as we often do fail to see it, what is good in itself can become harmful.

In *The Rare Jewel of Christian Contentment*, Jeremiah Burroughs speaks of a "fourfold burden in a prosperous condition": a burden of trouble, a burden of danger, a burden of duty, and a burden of accountability. Of these four, the burden he chiefly focuses on is danger: "Men in a prosperous position are subject to many temptations that other men are not subject to." Therefore, "a poor man who is in a low condition thinks, 'I am low and others are raised, but I know not what their burden is,' and so, if he is rightly instructed in the school of Christ, he comes to be contented."[4]

3. Elisabeth Elliot, *Discipline: The Glad Surrender* (Old Tappan, N.J.: Revell, 1982), p. 112.
4. Jeremiah Burroughs, *The Rare Jewel of Christian Contentment* (Carlisle, Pa.: Banner of Truth Trust, 1979), pp. 104, 107. Original edition 1648.

We have an excellent example of the danger of wealth in Christ's story of the rich man and Lazarus. The rich man did not perish because he had possessions; not a word in the story condemns him for his wealth. Nevertheless, we cannot escape seeing that there was some connection between his wealth and his neglect of those matters of mind and heart that would have led to salvation. He was rich in things but poor in soul, and it was his prosperity in the former that blinded him to his poverty in the latter, which mattered ultimately. This is the great danger of riches, namely, the desire to gain the world at the loss of one's salvation.

For this reason Hugh Latimer began one of his sermons before King Edward VI by quoting three times, "Take heed and beware of covetousness." He then added, "What if I should say nothing else these three or four hours?"

The Church of England prayer book, developed about that time, says, "In all time of our wealth, good Lord deliver us."

Possessions are dangerous because we tend to serve them rather than God, which means that things become an idol and our service of them becomes idolatry. Jesus taught this when He said in the Sermon on the Mount, "You cannot serve both God and Money" (Matthew 6:24). In the Greek New Testament the word Jesus used for "Money" is *mamon*, transliterated as "Mammon." It has an interesting history. Mammon comes from a Hebrew root meaning "to entrust" or "to place in someone's keeping." Mammon therefore meant the wealth that one entrusted to another. At this time mammon did not have any bad connotation. A rabbi could say, "Let the mammon of thy neighbor be as dear to thee as thine own." If a bad sense was intended, an adjective or some other qualifying word needed to be added, as in "the mammon of unrighteousness."

However, as time passed, the meaning of the word shifted from the passive voice ("that which is entrusted") to the active ("that in which one trusts"), and the concept became bad. Now the word, which was originally spelled with a small *m*, came (in English texts) to be spelled with a capital M as designating a god. The *New International Version* captures the idea by translating *mammon* as "Money."

This is what often happens with those who possess great riches. They may begin with a sense of having received their possessions from God. But instead of entrusting them to Him for safekeeping, they come instead to trust riches and thus idolatrize them. No one can do that and be Christ's disciple.

3. *Stewardship*. Central to any biblical understanding of possessions is the concept of stewardship, the principle that possessions are not ours to do with as we want but rather that which has been entrusted to us by God to do with as He wants, to be used in His service. It is the principle behind Christ's story of the landlord who went off on a trip and left his vineyard in the care of tenant farmers or the story of the master who entrusted certain talents to His servants. It is what Paul was talking about when he wrote young Timothy: "Command those who are rich in this present world not to be arrogant nor to put their hope in wealth, which is so uncertain, but to put their hope in God, who richly provides us with everything for our enjoyment. Command them to do good, to be rich in good deeds, and to be generous and willing to share. In this way they will lay up treasure for themselves as a firm foundation for the coming age, so that they may take hold of the life that is truly life" (1 Timothy 6:17-19).

The key idea is that earthly treasure is perishable. Frequently it fails to last even in this life. It certainly will not go with us into heaven. So what are we to use it for? The answer is that we are to use possessions to do good so that those good deeds will themselves produce treasures for us — not on earth, but in heaven, "where moth and rust do not destroy, and where thieves do not break in and steal" (Matthew 6:20).

People have a natural desire to lay up treasure in the sense of having what will last. That is not bad. But that kind of treasure can only be had in heaven and even then only if we use our possessions here properly.

I put the matter as clearly as I know how. The money you spend on yourself (which is necessary up to a point) will not produce treasure in heaven. It will be gone with the spending, and its benefits will perish when you do. But money you spend on others (which should be a rising percentage of your income, as God prospers you) — that treasure will last forever. It will be translated into eternal treasures to be presented to you at the Lord's coming.

Let me say it again, this time in language used by Dietrich Bonhoeffer: "Earthly goods are given to be used, not to be collected."[5] Wealth that is stored up will rot like yesterday's manna. Wealth that is given is like seed sown. It will produce an abundant crop for God's harvest.

---

5. Dietrich Bonhoeffer, *The Cost of Discipleship* (New York: Macmillan, 1966), p. 194. Original German edition 1937.

A HEART SET FREE

I close with an important thought. Wealth is a blessing when properly received and used, but there is something far more important than wealth or even the proper use of it. It is being free, as God intends us to be free. Possessions tie us down. Therefore, although most of us must have at least some possessions (and many of us will have a great deal), the only way to be really free is to hold those possessions as if we did not hold them and thus be ready always to let go of them at a moment's notice.

I am impressed with the way A. W. Tozer develops this from the story of Abraham's sacrifice of his son Isaac in obedience to God's commandment. As Tozer tells it, Isaac was the idol of the aged patriarch's heart. He was the son of a miracle, representing God's covenant, Abraham's personal hope of salvation, the promise of the Messiah, and much else besides. Tozer says, "As he watched him grow from babyhood to young manhood the heart of the old man was knit closer and closer with the life of his son, till at last the relationship bordered upon the perilous. It was then that God stepped in to save both father and son from the consequences of an uncleansed love."[6]

God told Abraham to sacrifice his son on Mount Moriah. What agony the command must have been for Abraham! It was an agony of understanding: How could God require him to sacrifice the one through whom He had promised to send the Messiah? How could God keep His promises if Isaac was dead? It was also an agony of obedience: How could Abraham go through with it? How could he kill his son? Abraham must have wished that it could be himself rather than Isaac who would die. His death would not be hard. He was old, and his death would be cheered by the last dim sight of Isaac, who was to carry on his line. But, no, the command of God said, "Take your son, your only son Isaac, whom you love, and go to the region of Moriah. Sacrifice him there as a burnt offering on one of the mountains I will tell you about" (Genesis 22:2).

Abraham must have struggled long and hard with the command. But he did not fail God's test. He cut the wood, saddled the donkey, made the journey, built the altar, and raised the knife to slay Isaac. It was only at that last moment that the angel of the Lord intervened to stop the sacrifice and commend Abraham be-

6. Tozer, p. 24.

cause he did not withhold even so great a possession as his son when God demanded him.

At this point Tozer pictures Abraham standing on the mountain strong and pure and grand, a man wholly surrendered to God — a man who had given God everything and who therefore "possessed nothing." Nothing? Yes, nothing! Yet Abraham was still rich. "Everything he had owned before was his still to enjoy: sheep, camels, herds, and goods of every sort. He had also his wife and his friends, and best of all he had his son Isaac safe by his side. He had everything, *but he possessed nothing.*" Abraham possessed nothing because he had first been possessed by God. He was the Lord's, and therefore everything he had sat loosely on him. Tozer calls this a "spiritual secret" that the books of theology do not teach but the wise understand.[7]

The reason God requires the renunciation of things is that the miser in each of us must be destroyed if we are truly to follow Him. His roots must be torn from the soil. Like the moneychangers in the Temple he must be driven out. Such action is painful. But when it has been performed, then we can begin to be useful. We can serve others by using things, rather than being used by them. We can travel light in Jesus' service.

7. Ibid., p. 27.

8

"But Is He with Us?"

"Master," said John, "we saw a man driving out demons in your name and we tried to stop him, because he is not one of us." "Do not stop him," Jesus said, "for whoever is not against you is for you."
— Luke 9:49-50

No one who does a miracle in my name can in the next moment say anything bad about me, for whoever is not against us is for us. I tell you the truth, anyone who gives you a cup of water in my name because you belong to Christ will certainly not lose his reward.
— Mark 9:39-41

Years ago I bought a car, and I remember sitting in the salesman's office while the final papers were being signed. I was surprised at how many there were. One by one they were all sorted out, and I signed whichever ones were necessary: a form for the dealer, forms for the state, documents authenticating the condition and mileage on the car, receipts for tax purposes. At last the pile was got through, and the salesman said, "Now for the personal part."

He was referring to my check for the purchase.

When we talk about discipleship, as we have in this series of studies, we are talking about the "personal" part of Christianity. Christianity has doctrines, which can be studied and discussed. It has history, which can be analyzed, applauded, or deplored. It has

buildings and ceremonies and organizations and budgets and leading spokespersons, and other things besides. These can be understood (and even participated in) in a detached manner. But not
discipleship! Discipleship is personal, which means that even a
study of it must be personal. That is why we have looked at self-
denial, personal obedience, service, humility, and "traveling
light" with one's possessions.

But although discipleship is personal, it is not personalistic, and
that means it also always involves our relationships to others who
profess to be disciples.

But Are They Disciples?

But are they really disciples? As I ask that question I am not referring to those people in the church who are essentially like us —
ethnically, denominationally, or in terms of our particular religious experience. We do not have trouble with these people, because affirming them is really just affirming ourselves. When I ask
the question, "But are they disciples?" I am referring to people
who claim to be disciples but who are different from us. I am asking: How should we regard *them*? What should our relationship to
these different disciples be?

This question came up during the days of our Lord's earthly
ministry and occasioned another of His important sayings. The
disciples had been arguing about who should be the greatest, and
Jesus had replied by an object lesson. He had taken a child and
had placed the child before them, saying, "Whoever welcomes
this little child in my name welcomes me; and whoever welcomes
me welcomes the one who sent me. For he who is least among you
all — he is the greatest."

The disciples did not always understand what Jesus was saying
when He spoke like this. But on this occasion John at least seemed
to understand. He remembered an incident that had taken place
not long before. He and the others had met a man who had been
casting out demons in Jesus' name. He was not part of their company, so John and the others commanded the man to stop. Since
Jesus had spoken of welcoming a little child and not offending
him, John wondered if maybe he and the others had been guilty of
doing that in the case of the independent disciple. He was not of
their number. He did not seem to have been authorized by Jesus.
But had they done right? John said, "Master, we saw a man driving out demons in your name and we tried to stop him, because he

is not one of us." He was asking, "We did right, didn't we?"

Jesus replied by a great statement concerning proper tolerance in religion: "Do not stop him . . . for whoever is not against you is for you" (Luke 9:46-50). He was telling them that the exorcist did not have to be among their limited number or in their particular association to be a disciple.

The Problem Explored

Before we draw conclusions as to what a Christian's relationship to other professed believers should be, we need to examine that story carefully. One thing we need to see is that although *in this case* Jesus said that the one who is not against us (and Him) is for us, it does not follow that there could never be a case or circumstance in which a mere professor could be opposed to Christ's kingdom.

One warning that this possibility exists is found in what on the surface is a direct contradiction to Christ's teachings. In Luke 9:50 Jesus declares, "Whoever is not against you is for you." But just two chapters later, in Luke 11:23, Jesus says, "He who is not with me is against me, and he who does not gather with me, scatters." These sentences seem utterly opposed; yet both are true, because they are speaking to different situations. In the second instance Jesus was speaking of the believer's conflict with Satan, showing that in that struggle there can never be room for neutrality. Some who were present were claiming that Jesus was casting out demons by Satan's power. In the earlier instance this was not the case. Norval Geldenhuys says, "It is a question of someone who believed in Jesus to such an extent that he cast out demons in his name and who revealed such a humble attitude that he allowed the disciples to forbid him to continue the work."[1]

In the incident we are studying the exorcist not only did what he did in Christ's name and therefore in open allegiance to Christ. He was also effective in what he did, for he was actually casting out demons. This indicates that his allegiance to Jesus was not in word only but by saving faith, for it is only as one is joined to Jesus by such faith that Christ's power is seen in him. In other words, the man was a true believer in Jesus. His action was a proof of his profession.

What was the disciples' problem, then? The problem, as John

1. Norval Geldenhuys, *Commentary on the Gospel of Luke* (Grand Rapids: Eerdmans, 1977), p. 289.

stated it, was that the man was not "one of us." That is, he did not
belong to the disciples' party. No matter that he professed faith in
Christ! No matter that he was doing good works in Christ's name!
He was not *of the disciples*; therefore they did what they could to
stop his ministry.

I am afraid we have become personal again. We are talking
about a disciple's relationship to other disciples and so have broad-
ened the limited concerns of our earlier chapters, but this nevertheless strikes home. Again and again in church history Christians
have denounced and persecuted others for no better reason than is
given here by John: "He is not one of us." They tell others, "You
must follow us or not work for Christ at all."

This is a devilish thing, for in extreme forms it has actually destroyed the gospel. I give two historical instances. First, it was the
error of Judaism at the time of the early expansion of the church.
The church in Jerusalem had no problem with Gentiles becoming
Christians so long as they also became Jews, that is, so long as they
became like those who had believed before them. But when the
gospel expanded to Gentile communities and the new converts
began to practice their own forms of Christianity, without reference to the laws and customs of Israel, a party developed that had
as its goal the conforming of the Gentiles to Jewish practices.
These people went to Galatia, among other places, and there
taught that it was not enough to be a follower of Jesus; a person
must be a follower of Moses too. It was not enough to have faith; a
person must also be saved by works. There was no salvation outside Judaism.

Into this arena stepped the apostle Paul, aghast that anything
should be added to faith as a condition of salvation. Salvation is
by faith in Jesus Christ alone, Paul argued. That is true even for
Judaism. For all his advantages, even the Jew will be lost if he adds
anything to the work of Christ for salvation.

The second historical example is the Roman church of the Mid-
dle Ages. The medieval church was orthodox in many respects. It
upheld the doctrines of the Trinity, the divine-human nature of
Christ, the atoning work of Christ, the work of the Holy Spirit,
the inspiration and authority of the Bible, and many other teachings. But something happened during those centuries. The Roman
church spoke of salvation through the grace of God in Christ, but
it came to think of the impartation of grace as something belong-
ing to the church and to be controlled by it. God displayed His
grace in the sacraments, but the church administered the sacra-

ments. So no one could be saved outside the Roman church. If you were to be saved, it had to be through baptism *administered by the church*, confirmation *administered by the church*, the Lord's Supper (the Mass) *administered by the church*, confession of sin to *a minister of the church* (followed by absolution), and eventually final unction *administered by the church*. Salvation was to be found nowhere else. So to be excommunicated by the church was to be severed from grace and so to perish eternally.

Luther was God's man for this hour, although the truth had already been declared by Savonarola, the Florentine Reformer. When he was condemned to torture and death in 1498, the authorities told Savonarola, "We excommunicate you from the church militant on earth and from the church triumphant in heaven." But Savonarola replied, "You may excommunicate me from the church militant here, but you can never excommunicate me from the church triumphant." That was exactly what Luther later discovered and proclaimed so forcefully. He proclaimed that one is saved by faith in Jesus Christ alone and that one does not have to be a member of the Catholic church or any other visible church to be a Christian.

Protestants are divided into many diverse camps, of course. So we are unlikely to make such extreme, erroneous claims. But we have errors enough of our own. We prize our denominational traditions and are inclined to think that no real good can be done in the world unless it is done by persons from our own particular confessions.

Bishop J. C. Ryle wrote,

> Let us be on our guard against this feeling. It is only too near the surface of all our hearts. Let us study to realize that liberal tolerant spirit which Jesus here recommends and be thankful for good works wheresoever and by whomsoever done. Let us beware of the slightest inclination to stop and check others merely because they do not choose to adopt our plans or work by our side. We may think our fellow-Christians mistaken in some points. We may fancy that more would be done for Christ if they would join us and if all worked in the same way. We may see many evils arising from religious dissensions and divisions. But all this must not prevent us rejoicing if the works of the devil are destroyed and souls saved. Is our neighbor warring against Satan? Is he really trying to labor for Christ? This is the grand question. Better a thousand times that the work should be done by other hands than not done at all. Happy is he who knows

something of the spirit of Moses, when he said, "Would God that all the Lord's people were prophets," and of Paul, when he says, "If Christ is preached, I rejoice, yea, and will rejoice" (Num. 11:29; Phil. 1:18).[2]

CAUSE OF DISSENSION

I suppose that in the entire history of the church there has never been a division, however unnecessary or sordid, that has not been justified by some persons on spiritual grounds. Yet if the truth be told, the great majority of diversions occur for base motives.

This is what is taught in the incident involving the disciples' rebuke of the man who had been casting out demons. There were two base motives. In each account of this incident (Mark 9:38-41 and Luke 9:49-50) John's question is immediately preceded by an account of the disciples arguing about who should be greatest and Jesus teaching them about the necessity of being a servant, using the example of the little child (Mark 9:33-37; Luke 9:46-48). In other words, there is a connection between these two happenings that teach that the disciples' basic problem was their pride. They wanted to be important. They were even jockeying for position among themselves. Hence, a demonstration of success by one who was not even of their own number was abhorrent to them.

Bishop Ryle wrote, "Of all creatures none has so little right to be proud as man, and of all men none ought to be so humble as the Christian."[3] Yet pride is often present even among the most serious Christians. The presence of this trait even among the disciples of Jesus should teach us that there is nothing against which we should be so much on guard.

There was also a second base motive behind the uncharitable judgment passed on the man doing exorcisms. To see this we need to go back one more incident in Mark 9 and Luke 9 and remind ourselves that immediately before this, when Jesus had come down from the Mount of Transfiguration with Peter, James, and John, the company had been met by a man who begged Jesus to cast a demon out of his son. He said, "I asked your disciples to drive out the spirit, but they could not" (Mark 9:18b; cf. Luke 9:40). Here

2. J. C. Ryle, *Expository Thoughts on the Gospels: St. Mark* (Cambridge: James Clarke, 1973), p. 190-91.
3. J. C. Ryle, *Expository Thoughts on the Gospels: St. Luke,* vol. 1 (Cambridge: James Clarke, 1976), p. 327.

is great irony. The disciples had failed to drive out an evil spirit. This should have humbled them and drawn them closer to Jesus to learn more about Him and to draw more closely on His power. But it did not. Instead, we find them arguing about who should be greatest and even rebuking another disciple for what they had failed to accomplish.

The disciples were motivated by jealousy and filled with pride. Is it not the case that this is what actually prevents much proper cooperation and interaction among Christian groups today? We criticize another group's theology. But is it not true that we are often actually jealous of what they are accomplishing? We need to deal with this sin if we are to go forward effectively in Christ's service.

One Body, Many Gifts

There is only one way we will ever defeat an improper narrowness in our view of Christian work, and that is to recover a vision of the greatness of the church as Christ's Body. We need to recover the truth Paul writes about in 1 Corinthians in his introduction to spiritual gifts: "There are different kinds of gifts, but the same Spirit. There are different kinds of service, but the same Lord. There are different kinds of working, but the same God works all of them in all men" (1 Corinthians 12:4-6). According to this and other passages, the church contains a variety of gifts, styles, causes, and methods of ministry.

1. A *variety of gifts*. The diversity in the church that the Bible talks most about is gifts, that is, the capacities for service given to every true Christian for the benefit of the whole Body. These are listed in five passages of the New Testament: Romans 12:6-8; 1 Corinthians 12:8-10; 12:28-30; Ephesians 4:11; and 1 Peter 4:10-11. The specific gifts vary in each passage, suggesting that the lists are not meant to be comprehensive but rather suggestive of the kinds of capacities for service God gives the church. The gifts are listed as follows:

1. Apostles (1 Corinthians 12:28; Ephesians 4:11)
2. Prophets (Romans 12:6; 1 Corinthians 12:28; Ephesians 4:11)
3. Service (Romans 12:7; 1 Peter 4:11)
4. Evangelists (Ephesians 4:11)

5. Wisdom (1 Corinthians 12:8)
6. Knowledge (1 Corinthians 12:8)
7. Pastors (Ephesians 4:11)
8. Teachers (Romans 12:7; 1 Corinthians 12:28; Ephesians 4:11)
9. Speaking (1 Peter 4:11)
10. Encouraging (Romans 12:8)
11. Faith (1 Corinthians 12:9)
12. Healing (1 Corinthians 12:9, 28)
13. Working of miracles (1 Corinthians 12:10, 28)
14. Ability to distinguish between spirits (1 Corinthians 12:10)
15. Contributing to others' needs (Romans 12:8)
16. Helping others (1 Corinthians 12:28)
17. Showing mercy (Romans 12:8)
18. Administration (1 Corinthians 12:28)
19. Speaking in tongues (1 Corinthians 12:10, 28)
20. Interpreting tongues (1 Corinthians 12:10, 30)

The mere listing of these gifts should encourage a measure of tolerance in Christian people, for it is evident that they are all quite different, that all (and perhaps others) are needed, and that none of us has more than a few gifts at best.

2. *A variety of styles.* It is not just in the gifts that we see variety. We also see it in the styles with which these gifts are exercised. In this area the apostles themselves are an example. Each of these men was given the gift of apostleship, but each was extremely different in his exercise of the gift. Peter was an effective, dynamic spokesman, who preached on Pentecost and many occasions thereafter. John was much more subdued. He traveled to Asia Minor where he died years later, being revered as a gentle and wise old man. Paul, who was called to join the ranks of the apostles later, was an aggressive evangelist. He would not always have been easy to live with, and we know that on one occasion at least he had a falling-out with Barnabas, another apostle.

Variety of styles frequently divides Christians today. But it does not need to. I do not mean that we will necessarily feel most at home with another worker's style. To imply that would be to deny the legitimacy of our own style. But I do mean that we should respect the other's approach to service. We should not use words like "superficial," "overly emotional," "cold," "shallow," "dry," or "introverted" to describe them.

3. *A variety of causes.* Many valid causes compete for a Christian's loyalty, but valid as each may be, no one Christian can be actively involved in all of them. The fight against abortion on demand cannot be every Christian's cause. The fight for equal access in the public schools cannot command all of every Christian's time, neither can the inerrancy cause or the battle to renew the mainline denominations or any one of a large number of other things. If this is so, we must not be critical of those who are involved in Christ's work but who are just not involved in the particular cause that concerns us. Above all, we must not expect them to stop what they are doing and come over to our particular movement.

4. *A variety of methods.* When I wrote of a variety of styles a moment ago I was approaching this area. But style is individual; method is organizational. When we speak of methods we are speaking of the difference between those who prefer to work within an institution to change it and those who prefer to work outside, between those who prefer direct confrontation and those who try to win by tact and persuasion, between those who work one-on-one and those who prefer to mount national campaigns. In any situation we may believe personally that one of these tactics is preferable to others, and we may be convinced that another believer is doing at least some damage by his methods. But perhaps we are too! He may be alienating people unnecessarily. We may be compromising. We are not to judge the other Christian, because he is not our servant. "To his own master he stands or falls" (Romans 14:4).

5. *A variety of places.* There are many places where work must be performed. I have been called to Philadelphia and am concerned about cities, Philadelphia in particular. I have preached on commitment to a particular place so much that I can hardly mention the word *place* without thinking along these lines. I believe in a commitment to the great cities of the world so much, and I want a commitment to Philadelphia by many Christian workers so much, that I can hardly stand to see a person go somewhere else. I am sometimes critical, especially when I see a person go to what I consider an easy, pleasant, or affluent area, particularly if it is for what I consider to be wrong motives.

But that is not right, of course. People are called to the cities, but they are also called to the country. They are called to the East, but they are also called to the West. They are called to this country and to other countries, to the poor and to the affluent, to working areas and to residential areas, to peaceful areas and to troubled areas. And it is good they are, for it is the entire world (and not just our own area of concern) that needs the gospel.

ARE THEY WITH US?

So I come back to my original question and ask of these other workers: "But are they with us?" The answer is that indeed they are — if they are faithful disciples of Jesus Christ. If we serve under the same commander, then we are all in one army. If we march to His drum, we are in the same procession.

But since *we* are asking the question, let us turn it around and ask it of ourselves. Let us not ask, "Are they with us?" Let us rather ask, "Are we with them?" We want them to back what we are doing, in spirit if not with their actual presence and resources. Do we do that for others who are equally serious about wanting to do good for Christ? Let me tell you one thing I do. I am often interviewed on radio or television and am asked about my work. That usually turns to a discussion of Christian work in cities. When this happens, and it often does, I never consciously allow the occasion to pass without commending other Christian works in Philadelphia, particularly the work of black churches. Their work is not my work. The styles are quite different. But I generally say, "The best work in Philadelphia today is being done by the black churches." And I give specifics as to the number of churches, the sizes of their congregations, the variety of services, and the quality of leadership these churches provide.

That is what we need to do for all who serve in Christ's name. We may not be able to endorse everything they do, but we should be able to say, "That person (or that work) is an authentic work of Christ, and I stand behind it. I am for any good work done for others in Jesus' name."

The Cost of Discipleship

9

Counting the Cost

Suppose one of you wants to build a tower. Will he not first sit down and estimate the cost to see if he has enough money to complete it? For if he lays the foundation and is not able to finish it, everyone who sees it will ridicule him, saying, "This fellow began to build and was not able to finish." Or suppose a king is about to go to war against another king. Will he not first sit down and consider whether he is able with ten thousand men to oppose the one coming against him with twenty thousand? If he is not able, he will send a delegation while the other is still a long way off and will ask for terms of peace. In the same way, any of you who does not give up everything he has cannot be my disciple.
— Luke 14:28-33

I was talking with a distinguished missionary doctor who was commenting on Christian work in his area of the world. According to him, there is much valuable work being done, and the people doing it are earnest and dedicated believers. But there is one thing lacking. "We want so much to win the people to Christ," he said, "that we are watering down the gospel to the point where believing in Christ hardly means anything. There is no repentance, no change of life. It is *easy* to become Christ's follower."

I was interested in this man's opinion, because, as I assured him, the same thing is true of much "gospel preaching" here.

One person who has challenged what he calls today's "synthetic gospel" is Walter J. Chantry. In *Today's Gospel: Authentic or Synthetic?* Chantry examines Christ's encounter with the rich young man, recorded in Mark 10:17-27, and concludes that his approach was radically different from what most evangelicals do in similar situations today. The man was clean-cut and earnest. He wanted to be saved. In that kind of encounter most of today's evangelicals would give the inquirer a three- or four-step presentation of the gospel, ask him to make a "personal commitment to Jesus Christ," and send him away with the assurance of salvation. Jesus did nothing of the sort. He first challenged the young man in regard to his conception of God: "Why do you call me good? No one is good — except God." He confronted him with God's law: "Do not murder, do not commit adultery, do not steal, do not give false testimony, do not defraud, honor your father and mother." Then he called for repentance and faith in Himself: "Go, sell everything you have and give to the poor, and you will have treasure in heaven. Then come, follow me."

Chantry points out that Jesus "demanded this turning from *everything* to himself as a condition of discipleship for everyone." Because it fails to declare this cost, much of today's church "isn't preaching Jesus' gospel!"[1]

What Is the Cost?

When a person becomes alerted to the teaching about cost in Christ's discourses, he is amazed at how extensive it is. Jesus did not make following Him an easy matter. Following Him involved radical life changes. Everything He said about discipleship implied this costly change. It was denying oneself, taking up a cross, and following Him (Luke 9:22).

Jesus also said many specific things about salvation's cost.

> Suppose one of you wants to build a tower. Will he not first sit down and estimate the cost to see if he has enough money to complete it? For if he lays the foundation and is not able to finish it, everyone who sees it will ridicule him, saying, "This fellow began to build and was not able to finish." Or supposing a king is about to go to war against another king. Will he not first sit down and consider whether he is able with ten thousand men to oppose the one coming against him with twenty thousand? If he is not able, he will send a delegation while the other is still a long way off and will ask for terms of peace. In the same way,

1. Walter J. Chantry, *Today's Gospel: Authentic or Synthetic?* (Carlisle, Pa.: Banner of Truth Trust, 1972), p. 55.

any of you who does not give up everything he has cannot be my disciple. (Luke 14:28-33)

According to this statement: (1) there is a cost to discipleship, (2) a failure to see this causes some to start out in the direction of the Christian life without adequate understanding and commitment, as a result of which they later fall away and perish, and (3) the cost must be paid if a person is to be Christ's disciple and be saved.

What a furor this raises in some evangelical circles! It is because the mention of "cost" sounds like a works-salvation, which is, of course, soundly condemned in Scripture, and evangelicals do not want the gospel to be destroyed in this manner. One writer says, "Any teaching that demands a change of conduct toward either God or man for salvation is to add works or human effort to faith, and this contradicts all Scripture and is an accursed message."[2] Such people rightly want to rule out any gospel that is not *sola Scriptura* (according to Scripture alone), *sola fide* (by faith in Jesus Christ alone), and *sola gratia* (by the grace of God alone).

But let us look at each of these distinctives.

1. *Sola Scriptura.* This means by "Scripture alone." It affirms that the written Word of God (the Bible) is the only fully authoritative rule for Christians. Particularly, it is supreme over any church or teachings or traditions. This is an important doctrine, of course. Protestants especially value it. But it is evident that if Scripture, being the Word of God, is supreme, then it is supreme not only over other people and other traditions but over me and my traditions. And this means that I must give up anything in my thought or practice that is contrary to Scripture if I would follow Christ. This is what the apostle Paul did. He said of his spiritual warfare, "The weapons we fight with are not the weapons of the world. . . . We demolish arguments and every pretension that sets itself up against the knowledge of God, and we take captive every thought to make it obedient to Christ" (2 Corinthians 10:4-5). We must pay the cost of the destruction of our own religious opinions to be a Christian.

Sola Scriptura also embraces the doctrine of repentance, for re-

2. From a book entitled *Handbook of Personal Evangelism*, by A. Ray Stanford, Richard A. Seymour, and Carol Ann Streib. The quotation is in Ernest C. Reisinger, *Today's Evangelism: Its Message and Methods* (Phillipsburg, N.J.: Craig, 1982), p. 31.

pentance means turning from sin (including sinful thoughts) to follow Jesus. It means renouncing and repudiating what we have thought but now discover to be contrary to God's revelation.

There is a great error in the modern church at this point. When the gospel is preached it is customary to speak about forgiveness, saying that we must confess our sin and turn to God where alone we can find forgiveness for that sin. That is true enough, of course. First John 1:9 teaches it. But what is equally true and yet not frequently said is that the gospel also requires repentance, which is not mere confession of sin but is a turning from it as well. The Greek word for repentance actually means a "change of mind." Repentance was the burden of John the Baptist's preaching: "He . . . preach[ed] a baptism of repentance for the forgiveness of sins" (Luke 3:3). When Jesus began His public ministry His own message was, "The kingdom of God is near. Repent and believe the good news!" (Mark 1:15). Later, the disciples "went out and preached that people should repent" (Mark 6:12). Peter declared, "Repent, then, and turn to God, so that your sins may be wiped out, that times of refreshing may come from the Lord" (Acts 3:19). On Mars Hill the apostle Paul said, "In the past God overlooked such ignorance, but now he commands all people everywhere to repent" (Acts 17:30).

On what basis did the early preachers of the gospel, including the Lord Jesus Christ, call for repentance and demand a change of mind? Solely on the revelation given by God in Scripture. What Scripture condemns must be repudiated. What Scripture commends must be affirmed. No one can have *sola Scriptura* without paying a cost in the intellectual and moral realms.

2. *Sola fide.* The second great distinctive is *sola fide.* It teaches that salvation is by the work of Christ received through faith alone. To protect this truth some teachers repudiate any thought of cost in obtaining salvation. But saving faith is not mere intellectual belief, as we have seen several times already. It is a living union with Christ, who is both Savior and Lord. It involves commitment to Him. No one can be a follower of Jesus who clings to lesser loyalties.

One cost we must be willing to pay in this area is loss of the world's good opinion. Bishop J. C. Ryle wrote of this in an excellent exposition of Luke 14:28.

A man . . . must be content to be thought ill of by man if he pleases God. He must count it no strange thing to be mocked, ridiculed, slandered, persecuted and even hated. He must not be surprised to find his opinions and practices in religion despised and held up to scorn. He must submit to be thought by many a fool, an enthusiast and a fanatic — to have his words perverted and his actions misrepresented. In fact, he must not marvel if some call him mad. The Master says — "Remember the word that I said unto you, The servant is not greater than his lord. If they have persecuted me, they will also persecute you; if they have kept my saying, they will keep yours also" (John 15:20). . . . It is always unpleasant to be spoken against and forsaken and lied about and to stand alone. But there is no help for it. The cup which our Master drank must be drunk by his disciples. They must be "despised and rejected of men" (Isa. 53:3). Let us set down that item last in our account. To be a Christian will cost a man the favor of the world.[3]

3. *Sola gratia.* This teaches that salvation is by the grace of God alone, with no mixture of human works added to it. "Ah," says someone, "that is exactly what we have been contending for: no good works. When you talk about the cost of discipleship, of paying a price for salvation, you are saying that there is something to be done, some work to be performed, without which one cannot be a Christian." No, that is not the point. In fact, it is a 180-degree distortion. *Sola gratia* means that it is precisely these good works that must be given up. The cost to the believer is his own self-righteousness.

This is a high cost to pay, and many will not pay it. When Dr. Herbert Mekeel first came to the pulpit of the First Presbyterian Church of Schenectady, New York, and began to preach the gospel as it had not been preached for many years prior to his coming, a woman who was a long-time member accosted him after a morning service. "Mr. Mekeel," she said, "I am leaving this church, and I am never coming back. No man is ever again going to call me a miserable sinner." She would not pay the price of her self-righteousness.

It is not hard to be an outward Christian. That costs hardly a cent. A person can go to church once or twice on Sunday and pretend to be tolerably upright during the week. He can serve on a committee when asked. He can sign his name to a pledge card

3. J. C. Ryle, *Holiness: Its Nature, Hindrances, Difficulties and Roots* (Cambridge: James Clarke, 1959), p. 71.

when the church or United Fund or some other charity is raising money. That even has rewards. We get a good opinion from others. There is no self-denial, no sacrifice here. If this kind of mere outward Christianity is all it takes to gain heaven, then, as Ryle suggests, we must alter our Lord's words to read: "Wide is the gate and broad is the road that leads to *heaven*." We must imagine Jesus saying to the rich young man: "You lack nothing. Keep what you have, and you shall have treasure in heaven too." We must suppose Him to teach, "You *can* serve God and Money."

Ryle writes,

> It does cost something to be a real Christian, according to the standard of the Bible. There are enemies to be overcome, battles to be fought, sacrifices to be made, an Egypt to be forsaken, a wilderness to be passed through, a cross to be carried, a race to be run. Conversion is not putting a man in an arm-chair and taking him easily to heaven. It is the beginning of a mighty conflict in which it costs much to win the victory.[4]

This is why Jesus urges us to count the cost and see if we are prepared to give up everything we have to be His disciples.

AVOIDING THE COST

The second point in Jesus' words about counting the cost is that many fail to think the cost through, start out in the direction of the Christian life with an inadequate commitment, later pull back in times of difficulty, and so perish. They are those in whom the seed of the Word is sown and in whom it quickly springs up, producing an interest in spiritual things. But the cares of the world later arise like thorns to choke it out, or persecutions like a hot Near-Eastern sun arrive to scorch it.

The Bible and life itself provide numerous examples.

When the people of Israel left Egypt under the leadership of Moses, thousands left in great excitement but did not count the cost. So when the traveling nation encountered dangers, deprivation, and delay they were discouraged and soon wanted to turn back. More than this, they complained against God and Moses, longing for the "leeks and garlic" of their former lives. All but a small number of the Israelites never reached the Promised Land. Many were judged directly and immediately by God. Thousands perished in their sins.

4. Ibid., p. 69.

When Jesus first came preaching the good news, many went out after Him and for a time appeared to be His followers. They marveled at His words. They were astonished at His power. They believed that Jesus was the Messiah soon to usher in the great age of Jewish blessing. But the more they listened, the more difficult and unpalatable His teaching appeared. They wanted Christ without repentance. So for want of counting the cost, as the Scripture says, "From this time many of his disciples turned back and no longer followed him" (John 6:66).

King Herod perished in this fashion. Mark says that Herod was impressed by John the Baptist and even enjoyed listening to him: "Herod feared John and protected him, knowing him to be a righteous and holy man. When Herod heard John, he was greatly puzzled; yet he liked to listen to him" (Mark 6:20). But Herod would not pay the cost of discipleship. He was living with Herodias, his brother's wife, and he was not willing to give her up. He cherished his sins and so died in them.

Demas found the fellowship of the gospel too costly. At the beginning he was impressed with the adventure of carrying Christianity throughout the known world, and when the apostle Paul invited him to go along on one of his missionary journeys, Demas must have been thrilled. It was a compliment to go with Paul. Alas, Demas did not reckon on the difficulties. So when the apostle was imprisoned, Demas began to long for the things the world has to offer and thus forsook both Paul and Paul's Master. Paul wrote, "Demas, because he loved this world, has deserted me and has gone to Thessalonica" (2 Timothy 4:10).

I fear that this is an all too frequent pattern today. Children of Christian parents, raised with a knowledge of spiritual things, frequently give verbal assent to Christianity. But the allure of the world comes along, and they discover that the cost of continuing with Christ is more than they are willing to pay. They want the world's glamour, the world's good opinion, the world's rewards. They drift away.

Products of an easy evangelism often do the same. There is a good evangelism. I am for it. Many are genuinely converted in mass meetings. But there are others — the best evangelists readily admit this is so — who start out as apparent followers of Jesus, perhaps genuinely moved by a sense of their own need and God's grace, but who do not follow through. Their unsaved friends pull at them, temptation beckons, and little by little they fall away. They are seen less and less frequently at meetings. Their attendance at Bible study becomes increasingly sporadic. Eventually they perish because they did not count the cost of being Christ's disciple and were never truly committed to Him.

Paying the Cost

The point of this examination of the cost of following Christ is not to discourage anyone from following Him, however. It is rather to encourage you to follow Jesus to the end. To do that we must count the cost, by all means, but then we must pay it joyfully and willingly, knowing that this must be done if a person is to be saved.

Bishop Ryle, who also listed the examples of those in Scripture who fell away from their profession, pressed his listeners to examine the religion they follow and turn from it if it costs nothing. He pressed them to turn to Christ.

> Very likely [your religion] costs you nothing. Very probably it neither costs you trouble, nor time, nor thought, nor care, nor pains, nor reading, nor praying, nor self-denial, nor conflict, nor working, nor labor of any kind. . . . Such a religion as this will never save your soul. It will never give you peace while you live, nor hope while you die. It will not support you in the day of affliction, nor cheer you in the hour of death. A religion which costs nothing is worth nothing. Awake before it is too late. Awake and repent. Awake and be converted. Awake and believe. Awake and pray. Rest not till you can give a satisfactory answer to my question, "What does it cost?"[5]

I challenge you to add it up. Make a balance sheet and list the cost; know what you are getting into. But at the same time list the benefits that Christ brings.

What must I pay to be a Christian? I must pay the price of my self-righteousness, no longer counting myself a good person but rather one who has transgressed God's righteous laws and is therefore under the sentence of His wrath and condemnation. But when I pay the price of my self-righteousness, I gain Christ's righteousness, which is perfect and imperishable. In that righteousness I can stand before the very throne of God and be unafraid.

I must pay the price of those sins I now cherish. I must give them up, every one. I cannot cling to a single sin and pretend that

5. Ibid., p. 81.

at the same time I am following the Lord Jesus Christ. But in place of my sins I find holiness, without which no one can see the Lord (Hebrews 12:14). I come to know the joy of holiness rather than the empty mockery of transgressions.

I must pay the price of my own understanding of life, of what it is all about and of what ultimately matters. I must surrender my confused and contradictory opinions to the revelation of God in Scripture. I must never attempt to correct or second-guess God. But when I do bring every thought into captivity to Christ, I find true liberation. As Jesus said, "You will know the truth, and the truth will set you free" (John 8:32).

I must pay the price of this world's friendship. I will be in the world but not of it. I will know that the world is no friend of grace to lead me on to God, but that it will always keep me from Him. Indeed, I must not only forsake the world; I must despise it for the sake of following after God. A hard price? Yes, but in place of the friendship of this world I have the friendship of Christ. He said to His disciples, "I no longer call you servants, because a servant does not know his master's business. Instead, I have called you friends, for everything that I learned from my Father I have made known to you" (John 15:15). Jesus is the Friend that sticks closer than a brother.

I must pay the price of my plans for my life. I have many ideas for what I want to do and be, but I must give them all up. I cannot both run my life and also have Jesus run it. Jesus is Lord of all, and unless He is Lord of all in my life, He is not Lord at all. If He is not Lord, He is not Savior. My plans must go. Yes, but in place of those flawed plans Jesus has a perfect plan that will both bless me and help others.

I must pay the price of my own will. That sinful, selfish will must go entirely. But in its place comes that "good, pleasing and perfect will" of God (Romans 12:2).

At the beginning of this chapter I told of a conversation I had with that missionary doctor who complained about the sad watering down of the gospel in his area of the world. At one point in the discussion he said that he had been thinking about what was the minimum amount of doctrine or belief a person had to have to be a Christian. He asked my opinion. I told him that a number of years ago I would have answered as I supposed the vast majority of today's evangelicals would answer. I would have said, "Well, it is necessary to recognize that you are a sinner and that Jesus Christ is the Son of God, who died to save you from sin. You must commit your life to Him." Of course, that is still a perfectly valid answer. Many millions of Christians have been saved by doing precisely that, because Jesus takes us where we are and teaches the fullness of what commitment means as we go on.

But I replied that when I answer that question today, I say that the minimum amount a person must believe to be a Christian is *everything*, and that the minimum amout a person must give is *all*. I say, "You must give it all. You cannot hold back even a fraction of a percentage of yourself. Every sin must be abandoned. Every false thought must be repudiated. You must be the Lord's entirely."

In this life you may go through days in which the world (and perhaps even yourself in low moments) will think that you made a bad bargain. But it is no bad bargain! The day will come in which you and the entire created universe will see clearly on which side the profit lies.

10

New Relationships

If anyone comes to me and does not hate his father and mother, his wife and children, his brothers and sisters — yes, even his own life — he cannot be my disciple. And anyone who does not carry his cross and follow me cannot be my disciple.

— Luke 14:26-27

We live in a disintegrating world. But in the midst of disintegration, no principle so unites people as family feeling. Dictators know this. They do everything possible to set husbands against wives, wives against husbands, and especially children against parents — all to increase loyalty toward the government. Quite frequently, when I am conducting weddings, I point out that the family is the most basic of all human institutions. The family was the first school; from the education that took place in the home all other institutions of education — grade schools, academies, colleges, and vocational institutes — developed. The family was the first hospital; healing and nursing originally took place within the home. The family was the first government; from a father's leadership in his home came patriarchal, monarchical, and eventually democratic forms of human rule. If the family stands, society stands. If the family falls, these other forms of social achievement and order will fall with it.

Christian leaders write about this at great length. I think of books like *Is There a Family in the House?* by Kenneth Chafin, *Christians in Families*, by Roy W. Fairchild, and *Heaven Help the*

Home! by Howard G. Hendricks.[1] These writers are worried about the family and want to strengthen it. Hendricks says, "The Christian home must blossom in a field of weeds."[2]

What right-thinking Christian would fail to echo that wish? What right-thinking *non*-Christian would fail to echo it?

It is therefore something of a shock to study Christ's words about discipleship and find Him saying what on the surface appears to be the very opposite. He says, "If anyone comes to me and does not hate his father and mother, his wife and children, his brothers and sisters — yes, even his own life — he cannot be my disciple" (Luke 14:26). In this verse Jesus seems to be tearing the home apart rather than strengthening it.

A Hard Saying of Jesus

This clearly is one of the "hard sayings" of Jesus, and it is hard in more ways than one. England's F. F. Bruce has written a book entitled *The Hard Sayings of Jesus*, in which this verse is discussed, and he concludes that it is hard for two reasons: (1) it is hard to accept, and (2) it is hard to reconcile with Jesus' other teachings. "The attitude which it seems to recommend goes against the grain of nature, and it also goes against the law of love to one's neighbor which Jesus emphasized and radicalized. If the meaning of 'neighbor' must be extended so as to include one's enemy, it must not be restricted so as to exclude one's nearest and dearest."[3]

One way of handling this problem is to regard these words merely as an example of Semitic hyperbole. Hyperbole is extravagant exaggeration for the purpose of emphasizing a point. If this is the case, Jesus is saying what in Matthew 10:37-38 He says in calmer tones: "Anyone who loves his father or mother more than me is not worthy of me; anyone who loves his son or daughter more than me is not worthy of me; and anyone who does not take his cross and follow me is not worthy of me." He means only that the interests of God's kingdom must be paramount among His followers.

But there are a number of reasons for thinking that this may be too facile a handling of the text. For one thing, it is probably not a

1. Kenneth Chafin, *Is There a Family in the House?* (Waco, Tex.: Word, 1978); Roy W. Fairchild, *Christians in Families: An Inquiry into the Nature and Mission of the Christian Home* (Richmond, Va.: Covenant Life Curriculum, 1964); Howard G. Hendricks, *Heaven Help the Home!* (Wheaton, Ill.: Victor, 1973).
2. Hendricks, p. 12.
3. F. F. Bruce, *The Hard Sayings of Jesus* (Downers Grove, Ill.: InterVarsity, 1983), p. 119.

proper interpretation of the word "worthy" in Matthew 10. We take that word lightly. *No one is worthy of Christ,* we think — and dismiss it. That is probably not what Jesus meant. When He said, "Anyone who fails to do so-and-so is not worthy of Me," He probably meant precisely what He says in Luke 14:26, namely, "He cannot be my disciple," which means, "He cannot be saved."

Second, the context makes Matthew's statement stronger than it first appears. It is true that in verse 37 Jesus speaks merely of loving one's father, mother, son, or daughter *more than* Himself. But in the verses immediately before this He says two very important things. First, He speaks of our failing to acknowledge Him before men, saying, "Whoever acknowledges me before men, I will also acknowledge him before my Father in heaven. But whoever disowns me before men, I will disown him before my Father in heaven" (vv. 32-33). That is speaking of salvation or a loss of it. Second, He speaks of bringing divisions to this world. "Do not suppose that I have come to bring peace to the earth. I did not come to bring peace, but a sword. For I have come to turn 'a man against his father, a daughter against her mother, a daughter-in-law against her mother-in-law — a man's enemies will be the members of his own household' " (vv. 34-36).

It is after this that Jesus speaks of loving a father or mother, son or daughter more than Himself. In this context the words in Matthew are not essentially different from the words in Luke. Both speak of a situation in which a person must choose between Christ and other persons (even members of one's own family). They declare that one cannot be Christ's follower without rejecting anyone who is opposed to Him or who would exercise a higher position of affection and authority in the disciple's life.

Luke 14:25-33 contains three sentences, each ending with the words "cannot be my disciple." The first says that unless we hate members of our families — yes, even our own lives — we cannot be Christ's disciples. The second says that unless we take up our crosses and follow Christ we cannot be His disciples. The third says that if we do not give up everything we have, we cannot be Christ's disciples. These are three ways of saying that we must count the cost in all areas and at all times if we would be Christians.

Beyond Accounting

In the last chapter I began with Jesus' words about counting the cost in Luke 14:28-33, deliberately passing over verses 26-27. It was because counting the cost was the more basic idea. Here, by going back, we go beyond mere cost accounting. We ask whether we are willing to pay the most painful costs for the prize of salvation. The statement batters us with four profoundly shocking truths.

1. *The radical demands of Christ's kingdom.* Over the years that I have been in Christian work I have been asked to serve on boards of Christian organizations, and to the extent that I have had time I have been glad to do so. I served on the board of trustees of the Stony Brook School for eight years and the board of an international ministry in Philadelphia for four years. I am currently on the board of directors of the International Council on Biblical Inerrancy, the Committee on Biblical Exposition, and Bible Study Fellowship. I have taken on those responsibilities willingly and enthusiastically. I have done everything I am able to do for these organizations. But I have not left father or mother or wife or children in order to assume these responsibilities. In fact, I have not surrendered any other legitimate responsibility to serve those boards.

Christ's statements about the demands of His kingdom are not like that. We think of most work as something that can be taken on and then later dropped (if it pleases us to drop it) with no great issues involved. But when Jesus presented the demands of His kingdom He always demanded the most radical commitment from His followers. It was not something that could be taken up and then dropped. It was not a part-time occupation.

Another way of saying this is that the coming of Christ's kingdom and the corresponding demands of discipleship were something utterly new in this world. Before this there had been people who had attempted to make such radical demands on other persons, but their demands were illegitimate. They represented mere human institutions, and the demands of mere human institutions are relative. As the Bible itself teaches, we owe the state obedience and loyalty. We must pay taxes to whom taxes are due and give respect to whom respect is due. But the state is not absolute. There are times when we must disobey it or prove false to God. The family also has claims on our loyalty, but it is not absolute. The claims of service organizations, political parties, and businesses are all relative. Not so with Christ's kingdom. The coming of Christ and His kingdom was something new in the history of this world, and its demands are beyond anything any other organization or movement can justify. Jesus made this point by contrasting His demands with the demands even of so high and honorable an institution as the family.

2. *The unique authority of Jesus Christ.* Jesus' statement that unless a person hates father and mother, wife and children, brothers and sisters — yes, even his own life — he cannot be a disciple, also teaches the unique authority of Jesus. For who would dare to say this unless He possessed unique authority? Who but God can make such demands?

This was the great issue confronting those who followed Jesus in the days of His ministry. When He began to teach they marveled, because He taught as one who had authority and not as the scribes (Matthew 7:29). When He quieted the storm on the Sea of Galilee, those who were with Him were amazed, asking, "What kind of man is this? Even the winds and the waves obey him!" (Matthew 8:27). When He forgave the sins of the paralytic the teachers of the law asked themselves, "Who is this fellow who speaks blasphemy? Who can forgive sins but God alone?" (Luke 5:21). It became perfectly evident to these and others that Jesus was speaking with more than mere human power and authority. Could He be God? That was the great issue. As we know, some rejected that conclusion and eventually crucified Him as a blasphemer and deceiver. But those who recognized His authority (substantiated by His miracles) went on to the inevitable conclusion and worshiped Him.

If Jesus is God, then the demands of His kingdom are more radical than we have hitherto imagined. When we hear Jesus saying that we must hate our fathers and mothers, wives and children, in order to be His disciples, that seems shockingly extreme. But if He is God, it is not extreme at all. If He is God, nothing He could possibly demand could be outrageous. If He is God, we owe Him total obedience and total self-surrender. Yes, even our own lives are not too much to give in His service.

On the other hand, the fact that Jesus is God makes the self-surrender all right. For God is not an arbitrary deity who has no concern for us, who, we might wrongly imagine, has concern only for His own self-aggrandizement. God made us. He has given us life and families and homes and a reasonable portion of this world's goods. These things are good because they are made by God and are God's gifts. It follows that if God requires us to give up one or more of these things in a specific situation — as a pioneer missionary might have to do in order to take the gospel to remote and

dangerous areas of the world — it is because the demand, hard as
it may appear, is nevertheless good in that particular situation. If
God is commanding, what is commanded is good for others and
for ourselves as well.

3. *The inescapable priorities of true discipleship.* As soon as we talk
of "good" in every situation or of personal sacrifice "in a specific
situation," we tend to relax, assuming that we are therefore off the
hook and that the disturbing radical nature of true Christian discipleship does not affect us. This is a false conclusion. It is true that
Jesus may never ask us to break with our families for His sake or, as
in the case of the rich young man, sell all we have and give to the
poor and then come and follow Him. In the great majority of
cases, this is not required. But *we must be willing* to obey in these or
any other areas if Jesus asks it. We must do it, if He does.

This is to say that we must get our priorities straight. Following
Jesus must be the most important thing in our lives, even more
than our lives. Nothing must be done that subtracts from that
commitment. Everything must be done to strengthen it.

George Eldon Ladd comments this way.

> The most radical form of . . . renunciation includes a man's very
> life; unless he hates his own life he cannot be a disciple (Luke
> 14:26). Obviously, this does not mean that every disciple must
> die; he must, however, be ready to do so. He no longer lives for
> himself but for the Kingdom of God. What happens to him is
> unimportant; for the fate of the Kingdom is all important. This
> is the meaning of the words, "If any man would come after me,
> let him deny himself and take up his cross and follow me"
> (Matt. 16:24). This does not mean *self-denial,* that is, denying
> oneself of life's enjoyments and pleasures. Self-denial can have a
> selfish end. By practicing self-denial men have sought selfish ad-
> vantage. *Denial of self* is the opposite; it means the renunciation
> of one's own will that the Kingdom of God may become that all-
> important concern of life. Taking up one's cross does not mean
> assuming burdens. The cross is not a burden but an instrument
> of death. The taking of the cross means the death of self, of per-
> sonal ambition and self-centered purpose. In the place of selfish
> attainment, however altruistic and noble, one is to desire alone
> the rule of God.[4]

4. George Eldon Ladd, *Jesus and the Kingdom: The Eschatology of Biblical Realism* (New
York: Harper & Row, 1964), pp. 295-96.

Some will think of this as a burden, but those who follow Jesus find it a liberating force. There is nothing so inhibiting as indecision. The person who knows what he is committed to can move forward decisively.

4. *The dangers of this world.* The fourth shocking truth in Christ's statement about hating father and mother, wife and children, brothers and sisters, is the insidious dangers of this world — even in the area of normal human relations and affections. We must say to ourselves, "If I can be kept from Christ by the normal love that I should have for parents, spouse, children or siblings, as Christ obviously teaches I can be, then how dangerous must the snares of this world be!"

When we speak of the world and its dangers we are, of course, not speaking of the world globe, the earth. We are not even speaking of the people who inhabit the earth necessarily. In the Bible the term "world" characteristically denotes what we would call the "world system." It is the way the world operates. It concerns the world's values and priorities. It is the preoccupation of the world with self and its pleasures rather than with pleasing God.

This is what must go, because this more than anything else is an enemy of true religion. Bishop J. C. Ryle asks,

> [Is it] not true that nothing damages the cause of religion so much as "the world"? It is not open sin, or open unbelief, which robs Christ of his professing servants, so much as the love of the world, the fear of the world, the cares of the world, the business of the world, the money of the world, the pleasures of the world, and the desire to keep in with the world. This is the great rock on which thousands of young people are continually making shipwreck. They do not object to any article of the Christian faith. They do not deliberately choose evil and openly rebel against God. They hope somehow to get to heaven at last, and they think it proper to have some religion. But they cannot give up their idol: they must have the world. And so after running well and bidding fair for heaven while boys and girls, they turn aside when they become men and women and go down the broad way which leads to destruction. They begin with Abraham and Moses and end with Demas and Lot's wife. [5]

5. J. C. Ryle, *Practical Religion: Being Plain Papers on the Daily Duties, Experience, Dangers and Privileges of Professing Christians* (Cambridge: James Clarke, 1959), pp. 187-88.

The world is sophisticated, persistent, and insidious in its temptations. How can we resist these temptations — if they can come to us even through the proper and desirable affection and loyalty we feel for members of our own families? The chief way is to be bold in confessing Jesus Christ.

During World War I one of my predecessors at Tenth Presbyterian Church, Donald Grey Barnhouse, led the son of a prominent American family to the Lord. He was in the service, but he showed the reality of his conversion by immediately professing Christ before the soldiers of his military company. The war ended. The day came when he was to return to his pre-war life in the wealthy suburb of a large American city. He talked to Barnhouse about life with his family and expressed fear that he might soon slip back into his old habits. He was afraid that love for parents, brothers, sisters, and friends might turn him from following after Jesus Christ. Barnhouse told him that if he was careful to make public confession of his faith in Christ, he would not have to worry. He would not have to give improper friends up. They would give him up. As a result of this conversation the young man agreed to tell the first ten people of his old set whom he encountered that he had become a Christian.

The soldier went home. Almost immediately — in fact, while he was still on the platform of the suburban station at the end of his return trip — he met a girl whom he had known socially. She was delighted to see him and asked how he was doing. He told her, "The greatest thing that could possibly happen to me has happened."

"You're engaged to be married," she exclaimed.

"No," he told her. "It's even better than that. I've taken the Lord Jesus Christ as my Savior." The girl's expression froze. She mumbled a few polite words and went on her way.

A short time later the new Christian met a young man whom he had known before going into the service. "It's good to see you back," he declared. "We'll have some great parties now that you've returned."

"I've just become a Christian," the soldier said. He was thinking, *That's two!* Again it was a case of a frozen smile and a quick change of conversation.

After this the same circumstances were repeated with a young couple and with two more old friends. By this time word had got around, and soon some of his friends stopped seeing him. He had become peculiar, religious, and — who knows? — they may even have called him crazy! What had he done? Nothing but confess Christ. The same confession that had aligned him with Christ had separated him from those who did not want Jesus Christ as Savior and who, in fact, did not even want to hear about Him. So it will be for you. Nothing will so keep the world at bay as a frank confession of Christ. It is the way to be His disciple.

OLD FAMILY, NEW FAMILY

I believe I hear what some may be thinking. "It is all well and good to be talking about breaking with old social acquaintances or other distant friends. But that is quite a different thing from breaking with one's parents or, worse yet, one's husband or wife. These are relationships that cannot simply be done away with, and any strain along those lines is painful." That is true. I offer this consolation.

First, it is often the case — indeed, it is generally the case — that God works in families and thus uses one who has become a Christian to draw his relations after him. It is remarkable how this happens. At first there may be great misunderstanding, even hostility. Parents especially tend to regard a child's new faith as a rejection of them and their values. But a change often occurs. Hostility is replaced by curiosity and then by respect for the new way of life. Conversations follow, and before long the parent, brother, sister, or others turn to Jesus. I have been a pastor for many years, and I have noticed something interesting. A generation ago the church was filled with parents who were grieving over an errant son or daughter. The parents were believers, but the children had rejected Christianity and were living the world's life. Today it is often the reverse. The children, often college students or young career people, have found Christ, and they are now concerned for their parents. Moreover, I have noticed that through the witness of the children many of these parents come to Jesus.

If you are having trouble with your family as a result of your attempts to follow Jesus, do not despair. Count it a temporary thing. You must follow Jesus regardless of what your family may say or do, but reason that the very fact that God has called you is encouragement to think that He may also call them. As Charles Spurgeon once said, you may be the "spiritual decoy" to bring them into "the gospel net."

Second, do not forget the wonderful new family God has given you through the work of Christ. You have much in common with the members of your natural family — similar personalities, shared experiences. But you have much, much more in common with your new family, the family of believers. It is what Jesus spoke of in Mark 10:29-30 (a text still to be studied). He declared, "I tell you the truth . . . no one who has left home or brothers or sisters or mother or father or children or fields for me and the gospel will fail to receive a hundred times as much in this present age (homes, brothers, sisters, mothers, children and fields — and with them, persecutions) and in the age to come, eternal life."

What a great family this is! It is one family because the members all have one Father. They have one mother, the true, invisible church. They have one elder brother, Jesus Christ. This is a happy family, because the members have turned from sin and are striving to obey Jesus. Pride is abhorred by this family. All rest their hope of salvation on what Jesus Christ has done, and they have no confidence in themselves. They read the same Bible. They go to the same throne of grace in prayer. They strive for the same gifts of grace: love, joy, peace, patience, kindness, goodness, faithfulness, gentleness, and self-control (cf. Galatians 5:22-23). They feel themselves to be at one with all other Christians. They have the same future expectations: the return of the Lord Jesus Christ and the establishing of His kingdom. They look to be united around His throne at the final resurrection.

Does the fellowship of Christ's cross cost? Indeed it does, but it has great compensations: blessings now and life in the world to come.

11

No Turning Back

No one who puts his hand to the plow and looks back is fit for service in the kingdom of God.

— Luke 9:62

Eight hundred years before Christ's day the prophet Elijah was led to enlist Elisha as his fellow worker and successor. He found Elisha plowing, went to him, and threw his mantle over him. Elisha immediately understood that this was Elijah's way of calling him to service, so he ran off after Elijah calling, "Let me kiss my father and mother good-by, and then I will come with you."

Elijah feigned indifference. "Go back," he said. "What have I done to you?"

Elisha would not be put off. He went back to the field, slaughtered his oxen, burned his plowing equipment to cook the meat, gave the food to his family and neighbors, and then set off to be Elijah's attendant (1 Kings 19:19-21).

Some have cited this story as one in which a servant of God put something before God's service: saying good-bye to one's parents. They have contrasted it to Jesus' words in Luke 9: "No one who puts his hand to the plow and looks back is fit for service in the kingdom of God" (v. 62). (The contrast seems apt, because one of the persons about whom Jesus spoke these words wanted to go back and attend to family matters after which he said he intended to follow Jesus.) Yet an examination of the two stories shows them to be in perfect accord. In Luke 9 the prior matters about which the would-be disciples were concerned were actually delaying tactics or excuses. In 1 Kings 19 the actions of Elisha were a demonstration that the decision he had made was irreversible.

In Elisha's case (as in the case of those who are true followers of Jesus) there was no turning back. Not only is the one who looks back unfit for kingdom service, he is not even a citizen of the kingdom. He does not qualify, now or for eternity.

THREE WHO FALTERED

Christ's words about starting out as His disciple but then turning back were a response to the excuses raised by would-be disciples, as I said. So it is valuable to look at these excuses for the types of distractions from service that Jesus says are incompatible with following Him. There are three. Each illustrates what Jesus elsewhere calls "the worries of this life, the deceitfulness of wealth and the desires for other things" that choke out the seed of the Word and make the individual spiritually unfruitful (Mark 4:19).

1. *Physical hardships and deprivation.* The first of these three individuals (like the third) volunteered to follow Christ. He said, "I will follow you wherever you go" (Luke 9:57).

There are many who have heard Christ or have heard about Him, often persuasively, but who have never got as far as this man got in his offer to follow Jesus. Many hear the gospel and are indifferent to it. Many are moved by Christ's call but never quite come to the place of starting after Him. Not so with this individual. He had heard Jesus teach, knew who He was, and was impressed by His person and message. He wanted to follow Him. But although he was sincere and was obviously moving in the right direction, he was a prime example of one who had not counted the cost of discipleship. He had not reckoned on the physical hardships and deprivation. So Jesus, who knows the heart, checked him saying, "Foxes have holes and birds of the air have nests, but the Son of Man has no place to lay his head" (v. 58). The story does not tell us what happened to this man. But since Jesus wraps up the three incidents by warnings for those who might turn back from following Him, we are right to suppose that this first individual did not pursue discipleship further. He was ready for a kingdom but not a cross. He wanted direction but not at the cost of deprivation.

He was like many would-be disciples today. If a preacher comes promising a solution to life's problems — "this world and heaven

too" — they are ready to sign on with Jesus. But speak of hardships and physical deprivations, and their enthusiasm withers.
Such "followers" do not follow Jesus to the end, and so they are
not saved.

We need to put down quite strongly that mere hearing of Jesus
and being attracted by Jesus will save no one. Bishop J. C. Ryle
wrote,

> The mere possession of religious privileges will save no one's
> soul. You may have spiritual advantages of every description;
> you may live in the full sunshine of the richest opportunities
> and means of grace; you may enjoy the best of preaching and the
> choicest instruction; you may dwell in the midst of light, knowl-
> edge, holiness and good company. All this may be, and yet you
> yourself may remain unconverted, and at last be lost forever.[1]

This does not mean that spiritual privileges are not true privileges or that spiritual advantages are not true advantages. The
apostle Paul spoke of Israel's advantages, saying, "Theirs is the
adoption as sons; theirs the divine glory, the covenants, the receiving of the law, the temple worship and the promises. Theirs
are the patriarchs, and from them is traced the human ancestry of
Christ" (Romans 9:4-5). But the people about whom Paul was
writing were not saved, and Paul wrote that he had "great sorrow
and unceasing anguish" in his heart for them (v. 2). Advantages
may *lead* to true discipleship, but they are not themselves discipleship. There must always be a personal following of Jesus Christ to
the very end.

2. Temporary but more pressing obligations. The second individual
in Luke 9 did not volunteer to follow Jesus. He was called by him
(v. 59). But he asked for delay, saying, "But first let me go and
bury my father."

Jesus responded, "Let the dead bury their own dead, but you go
and proclaim the kingdom of God" (v. 60).

At first glance this seems harsh of Jesus; indeed, each of these
calls is absolute and stringent. But the situation is probably not
what it at first sounds like to us. We think of the man's father as
having already died and of Jesus forbidding the prospective disci-

1. J. C. Ryle, *Holiness: Its Nature, Hindrances, Difficulties and Roots* (Cambridge: James
Clarke, 1959), p. 166.

ple even to attend the funeral. In light of Jewish culture of the time it is unlikely that this was involved. If the man's father had died, he would most properly have been at home already, mourning. Since he was not, it is probable that his father was merely old and that he was telling Jesus he would follow Him after his father died and this prior phase of his life was thereby ended. It might be years before his father died, but he would stay home for that duration. Jesus would not accept discipleship on those terms but demanded instead that the man come after Him right then and not delay his obedience to the call.

In the case of the first individual we have an example of one who failed to count the cost. In this second case we have one who was not willing to "hate" father and mother, husband or wife, children, brothers and sisters for Jesus' sake. Again, although the text does not say so specifically, we must assume that this person was unwilling to follow Jesus on His terms and so perished eternally.

Procrastination is a great enemy of discipleship. The one who procrastinates has heard Jesus' call and has acknowledged the necessity of obeying it. But other obligations press forward in his or her mind and crowd obedience out. The individual does not intend to delay forever. "Just let me attend to this small thing first," he pleads. But the delay of an hour becomes a day's delay. A day becomes a week, a week a year, and at last a lifetime has passed without any genuine response to Christ's call.

Charles Spurgeon knew many such persons in his day and wrote of them:

> You are only young apprentices at present, and when your time is out you think it will be early enough to attend to matters of soul-interest. Or you are only journeymen at present, and when you have earned sufficient money to set you up in business then will be the time to think of God. Or you are little masters and have just begun business; you have a rising family and are struggling hard, and this is your pretense for procrastination. You promise that when you have a competence and can quietly retire to a snug little villa in the country and your children have grown up, then you will repent of the past and seek God's grace for the future. All these are self-delusions of the grossest kind, for you will do no such thing. What you are today you will probably be tomorrow, and what you are tomorrow you will probably be the next day, and unless a miracle happens — that is to say, unless the supernatural grace of God shall make a new man of

you — you will be at your last day what you now are: without God, without hope, and a stranger to the commonwealth of Israel. Procrastination is the greatest of Satan's nets; in this he catcheth more unwary souls than in any other.[2]

3. *Determination to set one's own terms.* The third of these three individuals (like the first) also volunteered to follow Jesus. But he wanted to do so on his terms rather than on Jesus' terms. He said, "I will follow you, Lord; but first let me go back and say good-by to my family" (v. 61). On the surface this request is the closest of the three to Elisha's request of Elijah, which Elijah approved. But here the man's error is self-evident. He called Jesus "Lord." That is, he acknowledged Jesus' right of command over himself. Yet he was trying to set the terms of his discipleship. He was calling Jesus, "Lord, Lord," but he was not following Him in that capacity.

This greatly hinders and often eventually destroys many persons' discipleship. Not long ago I was in a meeting of ministers in which one was speaking of our lack of accountability to one another. He said that in his opinion the problem with most so-called Christians today is that they want salvation on their own terms. They say they believe the Bible. They acknowledge Jesus' lordship. But they will not make themselves accountable for how or when they actually obey Him. They want to control that response. If it is convenient, they will obey. But if not, they do not want anyone telling them that they are disobedient and are therefore not actually following Jesus. I believe that this is an accurate statement.

In his classic treatment of *The Cost of Discipleship* Dietrich Bonhoeffer has a careful analysis of Luke 9:57-62, in which he examines each of these excuses. He spends most time on the third since it is most critical. Bonhoeffer thinks the third man's excuse shows two failures. First, it reveals an inadequate break with the past. When Elisha went back to burn his farm equipment and kill his oxen it was to make that break clear and irreversible. He was a true disciple. In this case, it was the opposite. The man was clinging to old relationships and life patterns. Bonhoeffer wrote,

> The first step, which follows the call, cuts the disciple off from his previous existence. The call to follow at once produces a

2. Charles Spurgeon, "Scourge for Slumbering Souls" in *Metropolitan Tabernacle Pulpit*, vol. 7 (Pasadena, Tex.: Pilgrim Publications, 1969, 1973), pp. 554-55.

new situation. To stay in the old situation makes discipleship impossible. Levi must leave the receipt of customs and Peter his nets in order to follow Jesus. . . . The call to follow implies that there is only one way of believing on Jesus Christ, and that is by leaving all and going with the incarnate Son of God.[3]

The second failure is a lack of obedience. Obedience is essential to discipleship, disobedience utterly opposed to it. Yet many supposed followers think they can pick and choose where God's commands are concerned, obeying when they wish and disobeying what they wish. This is not discipleship. It is not even faith in Jesus as one's Savior.

Again, Bonhoeffer said that if one dismisses the word of God's command, he will not receive his word of grace.

How can you hope to enter into communion with him when at some point in your life you are running away from him? The man who disobeys cannot believe, for only he who obeys can believe. . . . Your orders are to perform the act of obedience on the spot. Then you will find yourself in the situation where faith becomes possible and where faith exists in the true sense of the word.[4]

Disobedience is really looking to something in the world, and if we look back, we are not fit to be Christ's disciples. Those who look back want to go back. Jesus will take no one on those conditions.

REMEMBER LOT'S WIFE

When Jesus said of these individuals, "No one who puts his hand to the plow and looks back is fit for service in the kingdom of God," He was not just making a statement, of course. He was giving a warning. It is this warning that we must now consider.

I turn here to another warning of Christ that must be taken with His words from Luke 9. This warning is found eight chapters farther on in Luke's gospel in a section dealing with Christ's second coming and the danger of being caught unprepared on that occasion. Jesus says, "Remember Lot's wife!" (Luke 17:32). This woman, wife of the Old Testament patriarch Lot, the nephew of

3. Dietrich Bonhoeffer, *The Cost of Discipleship* (New York: Macmillan, 1966), pp. 66-67. Original German edition 1937.
4. Ibid., pp. 73-74.

Abraham, is the classic biblical example of one who did not press on in discipleship but rather looked back and perished. She had been living in Sodom with her husband. She had been visited by angels and had been warned (along with her husband) to flee from Sodom, which was to be destroyed. She left at the angels' insistence. But on the way to the mountains she looked back in disobedience to the angels' strict command and was turned into a pillar of salt. Jesus said to "remember" this woman. Remember her advantages, her disobedience, and her frightful end.

We will never appreciate the force of this warning unless we realize that Lot's wife was a spiritually privileged individual. To begin with, she had a saved man as her husband. True, Lot was far from being a model disciple himself. He chose the cities of the plain with their seductive pleasures rather than the mountain country occupied by Abraham, and he paid for it. But Peter nevertheless calls him "a righteous man, who was distressed by the filthy lives" of the lawless (2 Peter 2:7). Lot's wife had the advantage of a saved husband, yet perished in spite of it. Lot's wife also had the advantage of a godly man's friendship, Abraham, to whom she was related by marriage. Abraham's faith would have been no secret to her. His knowledge of the true God would have been communicated to all who were members of his household, which Lot and his wife had been for many years. She would have participated in Abraham's worship of the true God. She would have seen evidence of God's power in delivering herself and the others who had been taken captive by Kedorlaomer and the other kings who had overthrown Sodom on an earlier occasion. Indeed, Lot's wife had even received the advantage of a special angelic visitation when the angels came to Sodom to warn her family. She was one of the small group of four whom the angels helped escape.

In that day not one person in many hundreds of thousands had such spiritual advantages. Yet in spite of her advantages Lot's wife turned back on the way and was judged for it.

What was wrong with Lot's wife? It is no mystery. First, she was disobedient to God's word through the angels. When the angels came to Sodom with the announcement that they were about to destroy the city and that Lot and his family would have to leave, the family was reluctant to go. The angels urged them, saying that they were unable to destroy the place until they were gone. Lot told his sons-in-law, "Hurry and get out of this place, because the Lord is about to destroy the city!" The angels said, "Flee for your lives! *Don't look back,* and don't stop anywhere in the plain! Flee to the mountains or you will be swept away!" (Genesis 19:14, 17, my emphasis). Those commands were as urgent and explicit as any found in Scripture. Yet Lot's wife disobeyed them. She began by delaying, dragging her heels. Delay then erupted into outright disobedience as she disregarded the angels' command and looked back.

Second, Lot's wife disbelieved. The angels had said that unless the family fled for their lives, refusing even to look back to Sodom, they would be lost along with those living in the city. But the woman must have reasoned as many reason today: "Surely God cannot mean what I have just understood Him to say. God will not really destroy the great city of Sodom. Or if He does, surely He will not destroy me just for turning around to see what is happening." But, of course, that is exactly what God did. God said what He was about to do, and He did it, as He said. Lot's wife perished for her failure to believe the word of God.

Third, Lot's wife loved the world and its pleasures more than she loved God. If you had talked to Lot's wife before the angels' visit and had asked her of her faith in God, she would have told you that she was a believing woman. She would have said — perhaps with an air of smug superiority — that she was not like the citizens of Sodom, who had no knowledge of God and were pagans. She worshiped the God of Abraham. She wanted to serve Him. She might even have told you what she was doing in Sodom to witness to the claims of this true God. She would have been one of the "better people" of Sodom. Still, her heart was not with God. It was with Sodom and its pleasures. Her true affections were revealed in the crisis of God's judgment.

Bishop Ryle has a magnificent sermon on this text entitled "A Woman to Be Remembered" in which he particularly underscores the danger of worldliness. He speaks of thousands who have begun well and run for a season but who turn back — not because they have found the Bible to be untrue or Jesus to have failed to keep His word, but because they have become infected with a love of the world and so serve it rather than the world's Master.

It is true of the children of religious families. It is true of married people. It is true of many young women and young men. It is true of communicants, even of clergymen. They begin well, but zeal for Christ grows cold, and at last they fall away.

Ryle wrote,

Beware of ever supposing that you may go too far in religion, and of secretly trying to keep in with the world. I want no reader of this paper to become a hermit, a monk or a nun; I wish everyone to do his real duty in that state of life to which he is called. But I do urge on every professing Christian who wishes to be happy the immense importance of making no compromise between God and the world. Do not try to drive a hard bargain, as if you wanted to give Christ as little of your heart as possible and to keep as much as possible of the things of this life. Beware lest you overreach yourself and end by losing all. Love Christ with all your heart and mind and soul and strength. Seek first the kingdom of God, and believe that then all other things shall be added to you. Take heed that you do not prove a copy of the character John Bunyan draws — Mr. Facing-both-ways. For your happiness' sake, for your usefulness' sake, for your safety's sake, for your soul's sake — beware of the sin of Lot's wife. Oh, it is a solemn saying of our Lord Jesus, "No man having put his hand to the plough and looking back is fit for the kingdom of God" (Luke 9:62).[5]

Onward! Onward!

The greater part of this chapter has been negative, warning those who are contemplating Christ's service that the mere setting out is not sufficient. There must be perseverance. It is he who "stands firm to the end" who is saved (Matthew 10:22). But I do not want to end there. I want to end on the character of those who are saved, those of "violence" who, Jesus says, "lay hold" of the kingdom and will not be denied until they possess it (Matthew 11:12).

It is said of Calvinists that they undercut all motivation for true godly living and evangelism. "For," the argument goes, "if God ordains all things, there is no obligation for me or anyone else to do anything. If God wants something to happen, it will happen. If He does not, it will not happen. There is nothing for me to do. I will sit back and let God work. I will enjoy myself and let it happen." That is not the way it is. It is true that in a way we do not fully understand that God does order the working out of all things. If He did not, He would not be God. He would be the victim of circumstances rather than being in charge of them. God is in charge of circumstances. But when God orders things He does so through means, and one of these means is the fervent persistent activity of those whose lives have been transformed by the utterly

5. Ryle, pp. 170-73.

divine work of regeneration.

Jesus told the educated Nicodemus that he must be "born again" (John 3:3, 7). If he was not, he could not even see the kingdom of God, much less enter it. Regeneration is from above. However, once the work of regeneration has taken place, the individual is no longer as he was. He is now Christ's man or woman. He is one who sees the kingdom and presses with all his might to enter it.

What is the character of those who put their hands to the plow and who do not look back?

It is the character of those who have an unquenchable thirst for righteousness and who will not turn back until their thirst is satisfied.

They have a hunger for spiritual things. They can never seem to get enough of God's Word. It is their chief delight all the day.

They are sheep who were lost but who have now heard their Shepherd's voice and are comforted by no other.

They were blind, but they have been made to see. Their eyes are filled with visions of glory yet to come.

They are pilgrims whose eyes are on the heavenly city.

They are virgins whose lamps are carefully tended and filled to overflowing.

They are servants who are using the talents given by their Master to the greatest effect. They do not bury them. They invest their assets in God's service.

They are people who feed the hungry. They give drink to the thirsty, shelter to the stranger, clothes to the naked, care to the sick, and comfort to the one who has been imprisoned.

They are branches who bear fruit.

Wells that do not run dry.

Runners who do not weary in the race.

They are servants whom the Lord finds watching when He returns.

Our earthly race is no sprint. It is a marathon. It is a marathon that begins with our conversion and carries on to the moment of our death or Christ's return. It is the hardest challenge we will ever face, but it is one we face gladly. For we face it in the power of Him who has promised to be with us to the end and who has said that we will never perish. No one will ever snatch us from His hand.

The Rewards of Discipleship

12

The Happy Christian

Blessed are the poor in spirit, for theirs is the kingdom of heaven. Blessed are those who mourn, for they will be comforted. Blessed are the meek, for they will inherit the earth. Blessed are those who hunger and thirst for righteousness, for they will be filled. Blessed are the merciful, for they will be shown mercy. Blessed are the pure in heart, for they will see God. Blessed are the peacemakers, for they will be called sons of God. Blessed are those who are persecuted because of righteousness, for theirs is the kingdom of heaven. Blessed are you when people insult you, persecute you and falsely say all kinds of evil against you because of me. Rejoice and be glad, because great is your reward in heaven, for in the same way they persecuted the prophets who were before you.
— Matthew 5:3-12

If a producer of a popular film, a director of one of today's successful television shows, or the editor of a widely circulating news or fashion magazine were to rewrite the Beatitudes from a contemporary point of view, I suppose they would go like this: Blessed are the rich and powerful, blessed are the sexually liberated, blessed are the beautiful and handsome, blessed are the famous, blessed are those the world looks up to. That is the exact opposite of what Jesus said in the Sermon on the Mount. He said, "Blessed are the poor in spirit, blessed are those who mourn, blessed are the meek, blessed are those who hunger and thirst for righteousness, blessed are the merciful, blessed are the pure in heart, blessed are the peacemakers, blessed are those who are persecuted because of righteousness" (Matthew 5:3-10).

Those words introduce the longest collection of Jesus' ethical teaching in the gospels and are a description of the life prescribed for those who would be His disciples. They unfold the essential call to discipleship: "If anyone would come after me, he must deny himself and take up his cross daily and follow me" (Luke 9:23). It is what "denying oneself" means.

The striking thing about the Beatitudes, however, is that the life they describe is not put forward as something gruesome or miserable (though necessary for gaining eternal life), but as the way to true happiness. For that is what the word "blessed" means. Blessed means "happy" — not in the world's sense of a mere superficial gaiety, of course, but in a deeper and far better sense. In the Beatitudes Jesus is saying that the cross is the way to real happiness.

Pursuit of Happiness

The world does not know this, of course. In the United States people are guaranteed "the pursuit of happiness" as an "inalienable right," and, like others the world over, they spend much of their time pursuing happiness. One man thinks that the way to happiness is through wealth. So he sets a financial goal of $100,000. He gets his $100,000, but he is not happy. He sets his goals higher. He thinks he will be happy if his net worth rises to $1 million. He gets that and starts on his second million, or his third. John D. Rockefeller was asked how much money is enough. He answered, "Just a little bit more." A person's desperate pursuit of money indicates that he or she is searching for something, but it also shows that money does not satisfy one's desires.

A Texas millionaire said, "I thought money could buy happiness. I have been miserably disillusioned."

A second man thinks that he will find happiness through power, so he goes into politics. He runs for a local council seat and wins the election. Immediately, even before he takes his seat, he thinks of becoming mayor. If he succeeds as mayor, he turns his eyes to the governor's mansion. At last he wants to be president. Power does not satisfy. One of the world's great statesmen once said to Billy Graham, "I am an old man. Life has lost all meaning. I am ready to take a fateful leap into the unknown."

Another person thinks the path to happiness is that of sexual liberation. So he divorces his wife, or she divorces her husband. The person enters the swinging singles scene where life consists of weekday "happy hours," Friday night cocktail parties, and over-

night weekends in the country. If a partner gets boring or posses-
sive, there is always another. Recently CBS did a television docu-
mentary on the swinging singles life style in California, interview-
ing one single woman after another. The women said, "All the
men want to do is get in bed with you. I've had enough of this to
last me a lifetime."

People think they can be happy by strengthening their bodies or
straightening their noses.

People believe they can become happy by writing a best-selling
book or by catching the attention of the masses through the enter-
tainment medium. Fame brings a sense of euphoria for a time, but
it is short-lived. The atheist Voltaire was one of the most famous
men in Europe in the eighteenth century. But as he lay dying he is
reported to have cried out to his doctor, "I am abandoned by God
and man. I will give you half of what I am worth if you will give
me six months more life."

Is no one happy then? Is the "pursuit of happiness" just a grand
illusion? Whatever the case may be with others, there was at least
one man who was ideally happy. We call him "the man of sorrows," and He was. He took our sorrows upon Himself. Still He
was happy. Billy Graham has written of Him,

> If by happiness we mean serenity, confidence, contentment,
> peace, joy and soul-satisfaction, then Jesus was supremely "hap-
> py." We never read of his laughing, though I am sure he did. He
> was not given to pleasure-seeking, hilariousness, jokes or poking
> fun at others. . . . His happiness [was not] dependent on
> outward circumstances. He did not have to have an outward
> stimulus to make him happy. He had learned a secret that al-
> lowed him to live above the circumstances of life and fear of the
> future. He moved with calmness, certainty and serenity through
> the most trying circumstances — even death! . . . Certainly if
> anyone had genuine happiness and blessedness, it was Jesus.[1]

In the Beatitudes Jesus tells how all who follow Him can have
that happiness.

THE WAY TO HAPPINESS

According to Jesus, happiness consists in a reorientation of life
by His standards. These standards seem contrary to our way of

---

1. Billy Graham, *The Secret of Happiness* (Garden City, N.Y.: Doubleday, 1955), pp. v, vi,
3.

thinking, as they inevitably must because of Jesus' holiness and our sin. But they are the secret — the secret to becoming a happy person.

1. *"Blessed are the poor in spirit."* In Luke's version of the Beatitudes the words "in spirit" do not occur (Luke 6:20). Therefore, many have used Matthew's version to point out that the poverty Jesus is speaking of here is not material but rather spiritual poverty. He is not praising physical privation. He is not saying that the materially poor are closer to the kingdom of God than the materially rich. What Jesus is commanding is the opposite of a person's being rich in pride. As I once wrote in an exposition of the Sermon on the Mount,

> Being poor in spirit is . . . to be spiritually bankrupt before God. It is the mental state of the man who has recognized something of the righteousness and holiness of God, who has seen into the sin and corruption of his own heart and has acknowledged his inability to please God. . . . The first of the eight beatitudes is one of the strongest statements in the Bible of the great doctrine of justification by faith in Jesus Christ alone.[2]

As I reflect on this Beatitude from the perspective of more than ten additional years of Bible exposition, however, I am not sure that my earlier explanation (and that of many other commentators) is adequate. I still believe that Christ's words speak of a proper, humble attitude before God. But I have also come to believe that it is impossible to have that attitude if we are clinging to possessions.

A disciple of Jesus is one who has renounced everything. He has no possessions of his own, no square foot of earth to call his home, not even his own life. The disciple of Christ is one who has died to self in order to live to God. True, he may have houses and land and family and friends (as Jesus even promises in the text to be studied next), but if he is a true follower of Christ, he will possess these things without their possessing him. A. W. Tozer wrote of this change,

> The blessed ones who possess the kingdom are they who have repudiated every external thing and have uprooted from their

2. James Montgomery Boice, *The Sermon on the Mount* (Grand Rapids: Zondervan, 1972), p. 23.

hearts all sense of possessing. These are the "poor in spirit." They have reached an inward state paralleling the outward circumstances of the common beggar in the streets of Jerusalem; that is what the word "poor" as Christ used it actually means. These blessed poor are no longer slaves to the tyranny of things. They have broken the yoke of the oppressor; and this they have done not by fighting but by surrendering. Though free from all sense of possessing, they yet possess all things.[3]

2. *"Blessed are those who mourn."* Mourning, like most of the other virtues in this list, suggests something spiritual. True mourning in the deepest sense is mourning for sin, and the comfort promised in this Beatitude is the comfort provided by the gospel. No happiness in the world compares with knowing that one's sins are forgiven and that fellowship with God has been restored.

But the text does not specify mourning in just this one sense, and there are two other ways the thought can be applied. First, it can be a mourning for personal loss, as is the case when one loses parents, children, a spouse, or friends for Christ's sake. Losses of this nature may be compensated, as Jesus promises they will be (cf. Matthew 10:29-30), but they are still losses, and there is still a genuine and proper mourning for the loss. Christ promises comfort for those who mourn.

Second, there is mourning for the world that continues to sin. Martin Luther translated the Greek word that occurs in this Beatitude by the German *leidtragen,* which means "sorrow-bearing." He meant by this that the Christian takes the world's sorrow on himself and bears it, just as Jesus takes our sin and bears it. The world will not bear its own sorrow. It is unaware of its impending disaster. Only the Christian knows the world's true state, need, and destiny. He mourns for the world. He also looks to be comforted as God uses our witness to draw many out of sin to Christ.

3. *"Blessed are the meek."* Western culture regards meekness as a despicable quality, like that of Casper Milktoast, who is always getting stepped on by the world. Meekness is actually a great quality. It is possible only to one who is far along in godliness. Here is a case where Jesus was probably borrowing from the Old Testament — from Psalm 37:11, which says, "The meek will inherit the land." This is important, because the earlier verses of the

3 A. W. Tozer, *The Pursuit of God* (Harrisburg, Pa.: Christian Publications, 1948), p. 23.

psalm delineate the character of the truly meek man. He is one who does "not fret because of evil men" (v. 1). Instead, he "trust[s] in the Lord and do[es] good" (v. 3). He "delight[s] . . . in the Lord" (v. 4). He "commit[s his] way to the Lord" (v. 5). He is "still before the Lord and wait[s] patiently for him" (v. 7). This is the Bible's portrait of the meek man. He bows low before God and therefore is able to stand tall before mere human beings, even when he is abused and persecuted.

Brother Lawrence was a meek man. He was not abused and persecuted, so far as we know. But he bowed so low before God, desiring to be his servant, that he was willing to do the kitchen chores in the monastery — and count it a privilege to serve in that capacity. He practiced the "presence of God" in his kitchen. So conscious was he of God's approval of his work that he could term himself "in all respects his favorite."[4]

There is a special promise to such people by which they may count themselves blessed: they shall "inherit the earth." The world may think such souls fit only for the kingdom of God, like the Emperor Julian who wrote mockingly that he only confiscated the property of Christians to make them poor enough to enter heaven. But Jesus does not say that they will inherit heaven, though they will. He says that they will inherit this earth, while those who currently possess it (He implies) will lose it all. How do they possess it? They possess it as the gospel spreads through preaching and God's kingdom comes. In the ultimate sense the meek will possess the earth when Christ returns, renews its face, and subdues all things to Himself forever. In that day the saints will reign with Him.

4. *"Blessed are those who hunger and thirst for righteousness."* In my study I have a book by Walter Trobisch, a German missionary to West Africa, entitled *Living with Unfulfilled Desires.* It is about adolescence and the postponed fulfillment of sexual desires that our Western way of life imposes on the young. This title might well apply to Western life in general. Only for most people these unfulfilled desires do not remain unfulfilled for long. Sexual desires are immediately gratified, or at least they are gratified whenever and wherever possible. Our culture tells us that we have a right to what we want and should seize it immediately. To use a

---

4. Brother Lawrence, *The Practice of the Presence of God* (Old Tappan, N.J.: Revell, 1958), p. 37.

biblical image, our culture encourages not a disciplined control of our desires but a hunger and thirst for everything. For everything but righteousness, that is! The world does not thirst for righteousness, since that is the one thing that is most perceived to stand in the way of the fulfillment of our other wants.

Yet Jesus says this is the way to happiness. The pathway of sin promises fulfillment; it promises to lead us through Elysian fields of happiness. It actually dead-ends in the "slough of despond." The path of righteousness seems hard, but it leads to true contentment. David knew that and wrote, "You have made known to me the path of life; you will fill me with joy in your presence, with eternal pleasures at your right hand" (Psalm 16:11).

But we must *hunger* and *thirst* for righteousness — as intently as those who hunger and thirst for this world's pleasures. E. M. Blaiklock wrote an article for *Eternity* magazine on the significance of water in the Bible in which he dramatically portrayed how intense a desire for water can be in desert lands and how a similar desire must fill God's people. His point came from an account of part of the British liberation of Palestine in World War I as described by Major V. Gilbert in *The Last Crusade*.

> Driving up from Beersheba, a combined force of British, Australians and New Zealanders were pressing on the rear of the Turkish retreat over arid desert. The attack outdistanced its water-carrying camel train. Water bottles were empty. The sun blazed pitilessly out of a sky where the vultures wheeled expectantly.
>
> "Our heads ached," writes Gilbert, "and our eyes became bloodshot and dim in the blinding glare. . . . Our tongues began to swell. . . . Our lips turned a purplish black and burst." Those who dropped out of the column were never seen again, but the desperate force battled on to Sheria. There were wells at Sheria, and had they been unable to take the place by nightfall, thousands were doomed to die of thirst. "We fought that day," writes Gilbert, "as men fight for their lives. . . . We entered Sheria station on the heels of the retreating Turks. The first objects which met our view were the great stone cisterns full of cold, clear, drinking water. In the still night air the sound of water running into the tanks could be distinctly heard, maddening in its nearness; yet not a man murmured when orders were given for the battalions to fall in, two deep, facing the cisterns."
>
> He then describes the stern priorities: the wounded, those on guard duty, then company by company. It took four hours before the last man had his drink of water, and in all that time they had been standing twenty feet from a low stone wall on the

other side of which were thousands of gallons of water.

"I believe," Major Gilbert concludes, "that we all learned our first real Bible lesson on that march from Beersheba to Sheria wells." If such were our thirst for God, for righteousness, for his will in our life, a consuming, all-embracing, preoccupying desire, how rich in the fruits of the Spirit would we be.[5]

5. *"Blessed are the merciful."* Each of the Beatitudes describes the character of the person who is following Christ, but there is a progression. The first three characteristics — poverty of spirit, mourning for sin, and meekness before God — show how one must approach God in order to find true happiness. The fourth Beatitude, the central and chief one, shows the fulfillment of the most important of all desires, the desire for righteousness, by Christ. At this point, the Beatitudes turn from the approach and fulfillment to the fruit, showing the transformed character of the one who has been touched by Christ's Spirit and is now being transformed into His image. They speak of mercy, purity, and a working disposition for peace.

Mercy is the first characteristic. It may be defined as grace in action. It is love reaching out to those who actually deserve God's judgment. This is a characteristic of God, and it is most clearly seen at Christ's cross.

I think Bonhoeffer is right when he contrasts the showing of mercy with the defense of our own supposed dignity. True, there is a proper dignity that everyone made in the image of God has, just by being made in God's image. But there is also a wrong sense of dignity or at least a wrong use of it. It is the dignity that tells us that we are too good to mingle with those below our station or too important to spend time with those who are not with it or are still on the way up. It is a sinful dignity born of pride. Bonhoeffer writes,

> These men without possessions or power, these strangers on the earth, these sinners, these followers of Jesus, have in their life with him *renounced their own dignity*, for they are merciful. . . . They take upon themselves the distress and humiliation and sin of others. They have an irresistible love for the down-trodden, the sick, the wretched, the wronged, the outcast and all who are tortured with anxiety. . . . If any man falls into disgrace, the

5. E. M. Blaiklock, "New Light on Bible Imagery: Water," *Eternity,* August 1966, pp. 27-29.

merciful will sacrifice their own honor to shield him, and take his shame upon themselves. They will be found consorting with publicans and sinners, careless of the shame they incur thereby.[6]

The promise to those who show mercy is that they will find mercy. Indeed, they have already found it and are blessed thereby.

6. *"Blessed are the pure in heart."* There was a time in Western culture when purity was valued, at least verbally. No longer! Today it is considered foolish, "puritanical," or unsophisticated to be pure. Virginity is despised. Honesty is considered passe. Are we happier for this new, "liberated" morality? We may say so, but the anxiety, grief, and frustration of our contemporary society belies the profession. Jesus said that the way to happiness is by purity, and it is easy to see why. Sin produces turmoil. Isaiah wrote, "The wicked are like the tossing sea, which cannot rest, whose waves cast up mire and mud. 'There is no peace,' says my God, 'for the wicked' " (Isaiah 57:20-21). God gives peace to those who seek purity. The promise of this Beatitude is that at the last they shall see Him.

7. *"Blessed are the peacemakers."* Not only do the followers of Christ find peace within through the pursuit of purity, they seek to promote peace with and among others also. Why? Because they are at peace themselves and know the blessing of it. The followers of Christ have been at war with God, and because they have been at war with God they have also been at war with others and themselves. Breaking the vertical relationship breaks horizontal ties. Now these followers of Jesus have peace. *They* did not make it. God made peace with them through Christ's cross. Paul wrote, "In Christ Jesus you who once were far away have been brought near through the blood of Christ. For he himself is our peace" (Ephesians 2:13-14). Having found a true and permanent peace with God, they now seek to establish and maintain a similar peace with others.

Bonhoeffer writes, "The followers of Jesus . . . maintain fellowship where others would break if off. They renounce all self-assertion and quietly suffer in the face of hatred and wrong. In so doing they overcome evil with good and establish the peace of God in a

6. Dietrich Bonhoeffer, *The Cost of Discipleship* (New York: Macmillan, 1966), pp. 124-25. Original German edition 1937.

world of war and hate."[7]

8. *"Blessed are those who are persecuted because of righteousness."*
The last of the Beatitudes speaks of happiness in persecution. This
is a blessedness Jesus elaborates upon, adding in verses 11 and 12,
"Blessed are you when people insult you, persecute you and falsely
say all kinds of evil against you because of me. Rejoice and be
glad, because great is your reward in heaven, for in the same way
they persecuted the prophets who were before you."

At no point in the entire list of Beatitudes is it more necessary
to know precisely what Jesus says than here, for it is not just any
kind of suffering that Jesus blesses. It is not persecution for wrong-
doing; that should be obvious. It is not persecution for being fa-
natical, as some who profess the name of Christ have been. It is
not persecution for being a nuisance; some believers have plagued
their neighbors in an effort to witness to them and have been
scorned for that. It is not even persecution for a cause, however
important the cause may be. There is only one kind of persecution
this Beatitude refers to, and that is persecution that comes to believers from being like the Lord Jesus Christ, whom they are following. Verse 10 calls it persecution "because of righteousness."
Verse 11 calls it persecution "because of me [that is, because of Je-
sus]." It is by being like Him and suffering for it in a world that
hates Christ that we find happiness.

How is this so? How can any persecution, even persecution of
this nature, make one happy? It promotes our happiness because it
shows that we are united to Christ, like that great host of "saints,
apostles, prophets, martyrs" that have gone before us, and that we
are growing in Christ's likeness. Jesus said, "If you belonged to the
world, it would love you as its own. As it is, you do not belong to
the world, but I have chosen you out of the world. That is why the
world hates you" (John 15:19).

IMITATION OF CHRIST

I end with this question. Where in this great world in which we
live can there be found a place for those who imitate the Lord Jesus Christ and thus in their own persons live out the Beatitudes?
This is not an easy world. It is a tough, hard, grasping, evil, covet-
ous world. Where can there possibly be a place for those who are

7. Ibid., p. 126.

poor in spirit, who mourn for sin, who are meek, who hunger and thirst for righteousness (of all things), who are merciful, who are pure in heart, who are peacemakers, who are persecuted for Jesus' sake? There is only one place. It is the place the great of this world assigned Christ. It is the cross. That is where the imitation of Christ is practiced, and it is why that imitation of Christ is the fellowship of the cross. The world cries to us, as it cried to Jesus, "Away with them; they are not fit to live." But as we are driven away, we are driven to Him whose very glance is precious above rubies and the knowledge of whom is life eternal.

We are driven to the fellowship of God. It is only at the cross that the gulf between a holy God and sinful man is bridged, sin is removed, and a wide channel for the fullness of God's blessing is unclogged. As we draw near to Jesus we hear the world's shrill cries: "Crucify him; crucify them." We hear Jesus as He speaks words of blessing and know ourselves blessed. "Blessed are you," says Jesus. "Rejoice and be glad, because great is your reward in heaven. In the same way they persecuted the prophets who were before you."

At the cross all tears are wiped away.

At the cross we find Jesus who is the fountain of all happiness.

13

Present Blessings, Plus Persecutions

I tell you the truth, . . . no one who has left home or brothers or sisters or mother or father or children or fields for me and the gospel will fail to receive a hundred times as much in this present age (homes, brothers, sisters, mothers, children and fields — and with them persecutions) and in the age to come, eternal life.

— Mark 10:29-30

Since God's ways are not our ways it is natural for us to be surprised by Christ's sayings. Yet in this great collection of unexpected and challenging teachings about discipleship by Jesus there is perhaps nothing so utterly unexpected (particularly after our study of the earlier sayings) as Jesus' words in Mark 10:29-30. All along Jesus had been telling His listeners that in order to be His disciples they must deny themselves and give over everything they possess. But now He says that if they do that they will nevertheless receive a hundred times as much as was given up, not merely in some future life, which we might expect, but in this very age — though they would have persecutions.

Jesus said, "I tell you the truth, . . . no one who has left home or brothers or sisters or mother or father or children or fields for me and the gospel will fail to receive a hundred times as much in this present age (homes, brothers, sisters, mothers, children and fields — and with them, persecutions) and in the age to come, eternal life."

An Astonishing Statement

This statement becomes more astonishing as we study it. It is surprising that it speaks of rewards, first of all, since there is nothing in the mere notion of discipleship that requires them. (At best we are unprofitable servants.) However, in addition to speaking of rewards (perhaps spiritual rewards would suffice), it speaks specifically of homes, brothers, sisters, mothers, fathers, children and fields — and these not in reference to some far-off heavenly realm, but in "this present age."

Mention of "fields" is most interesting. The other terms can be spiritualized to an extent. When Jesus mentioned "homes" He is, I believe, speaking of literal earthly homes, involving family members and houses and furniture and pots and pans and such things. But it might be possible to think instead of a "heavenly home" and thus remove this element from earthly life. The same might be done with brothers, sisters, mothers, fathers, and children. These might be referring merely to the "family of God" in heaven. This cannot be done with "fields." Fields have to do with earth. Thus, the mention of fields alone carries us back to the context, in which earthly possessions are discussed, and warns us about taking any of the other elements of this promise "spiritually."

The preceding verses tell the story of the rich young man, Jesus' words to him, and Peter's response to Christ. The young man had come wanting to follow Jesus, but when he was warned that riches were standing in the way of true discipleship "he went away sad, because he had great wealth" (v. 22). This caused Jesus to comment on how hard it is for the rich to enter the kingdom of God (vv. 23-24).

Apparently the young man was not the only one who was sad. He was despondent because he could not follow Jesus and retain his possessions too. But Jesus also was sad because of his leaving, and Peter, noticing this, tried to cheer the Lord up. The young man had gone away, but Jesus still had His disciples, Peter thought. So he said, "*We* have left everything to follow you!" (v. 28, my emphasis). In response to this Jesus instructed the disciples further, using the words we are studying. Thus, the saying must refer not to some heavenly, spiritual reward (though there is that too) but to Christ's provision of families and possessions for His followers in this age. The statement is qualified — possessions are to be accompanied by persecutions — but it deals with possessions nonetheless.

Most astonishing of all, the disciples were to receive *a hundred times* as much of these things as they had previously possessed. We remember that even Job received only double his possessions after God restored him to prosperity!

We must exercise some caution at this point, of course. For one thing, nothing in Christ's teachings would encourage us to think of this in crass materialistic terms, as if Jesus were merely giving a formula for sure wealth. Even this saying is ludicrous if taken in that way. If this is a formula for wealth, then what we should do is, first, earn all we can (taking years to do it if necessary), second, give up those earnings for Jesus, and then wait for Jesus to multiply the gift by one hundred. That would discourage discipleship rather than promote it. Again, this promise does not necessarily apply to every individual. It is clear that some believers (though not all) are called to poverty. No matter how much they have and give up, they will always have only the most modest means, because that is what God has called them to have. I suppose that most of the disciples were in this category.

However, the text is a great promise, and it does have to do with earthly relationships and material possessions. At the least, it means that the true follower of Christ will not lack for any good thing ("My cup overflows," Psalm 23:6) and that, in normal circumstances, a Christian will be blessed with earthly good abundantly. Personally I am convinced that Jesus gives us every good that He can possibly give us without rendering us unfit for His work or destroying our souls. The reason many of us do not have more is that the Lord knows we would misuse it.

ENCOURAGEMENT TO SERVE

In spite of these obvious qualifications, Christ's promise of homes, family, and fields is an encouragement to those willing to serve Him. Basically it tells us that God is good and that He is no man's debtor. Sometimes the idea that "God is no man's debtor" has been used wrongly to try to control God, as it were. People have suggested that if we do so-and-so, then God is obligated to do so-and-so for us. That is manipulative; the text does not support this view. However, properly received, it does encourage us to serve God in Christ's service, knowing that we will be blessed for it. There are several important grounds for this encouragement.

1. *Greater blessings.* One thing that keeps many from following

Jesus — the rich young ruler is an example — is the feeling that the cost of following Him is too high. We would have to give up "too much." Mark 10:29-30 teaches that the blessings to be found in Christ's service are greater than the blessings we could have without it. The rich young man was unwilling to give up his possessions. He loved them more than he loved Jesus, and he could not be saved without loving God with all his heart and soul and mind and strength. However, if he had followed Christ, turning his back on his wealth, what this text clearly teaches is that Jesus would have blessed him a hundred times over with a home, family, and lands. He could not be certain of the form Christ's blessing would take. He might have been called to a life of itinerant ministry, as Paul was called. But whatever form of his service, the blessings he would receive in that service (even great material possessions) would be many times greater than anything he could have given up.

One must address Christians and not unbelievers to get a true perspective on this promise.

Abraham, were you cheated by Jesus when you forsook everything to follow Him? You left the good land of Ur. You left family, home, and fields to become a pilgrim in the earth. Wasn't that a bad bargain? Weren't you cheated here, regardless of what may or may not be true in heaven?

Abraham answers, "Cheated? How could I possibly be cheated? It is true that I left houses and family and land to follow God's call, but I received a hundred times more than ever I gave up. God gave me a great family, so much so that on one occasion I was able to gather 318 trained men born in my own household to go and fight against the kings of the East commanded by Kedorlaomer, king of Elam. And, of course, I became the father of that great family of God that even now numbers as many persons as grains of sand on the seashore or the stars of heaven. So far as land is concerned, it is true that I only owned one small parcel of land: the land containing the cave where I buried Sarah. But during my day I roamed over the entire land of Canaan as if it were mine, and in time it was all given to my descendants."

Moses, you are another of God's choice servants. You forsook Egypt with its pleasures and wealth to obey God in leading a nation of slaves through the desert. You died in the desert. Wouldn't you say that you had made a bad bargain?

Moses answers, "A bad bargain? Not at all! It is true that I left Egypt, regarding 'disgrace for the sake of Christ as of greater value than the treasures of Egypt,' but I did so because I was 'looking ahead to [my] reward,' " as the author of Hebrews says [Hebrews 11:26]. I received a great nation as my family — in addition to a natural family of my own. I saw the Promised Land and even received it by faith. Most important, I saw God, and in comparison with that blessing nothing else ever really matters."

We won't ask you, David. We know what you'll say. You'll say that God took you from following the sheep and made you the greatest of Israel's kings. You had many wives, children, palaces, and fields. But let's talk to Gideon, Barak, Samson, Jephthath, Samuel, and the prophets.

The Bible says that these "through faith conquered kingdoms, administered justice, and gained what was promised" (Hebrews 11:33).

Talk to Paul. Paul wrote, "It seems to me that God has put us apostles on display at the end of the procession, like men condemned to die in the arena. We have been made a spectacle to the whole universe, to angels as well as to men. We are fools for Christ. . . . We are weak. . . . We are dishonored! To this very hour we go hungry and thirsty, we are in rags, we are brutally treated, we are homeless" (1 Corinthians 4:9-11). Paul said,

> Five times I received from the Jews the forty lashes minus one. Three times I was beaten with rods, once I was stoned, three times I was shipwrecked, I spent a night and a day in the open sea, I have been constantly on the move. I have been in danger from rivers, in danger from bandits, in danger from my own countrymen, in danger from Gentiles; in danger in the city, in danger in the country, in danger at sea; and in danger from false brothers. I have labored and toiled and have often gone without sleep; I have known hunger and thirst and have often gone without food; I have been cold and naked. Besides everything else, I face daily the pressure of my concern for all the churches. (2 Corinthians 11:24-28)

Does that sound like material rewards? Does that sound like homes, family, and fields in great measure?

It is true that Paul (like the other apostles) was chosen to be a spectacle of great suffering, but even he does not call discipleship a bad bargain. While in prison he wrote, "I have received full payment and even more; I am amply supplied" (Philippians 4:18).

Not one of the apostles would ever have considered his decision to follow Christ unfortunate.

2. *Certain blessings.* It is not only the greatness of the blessings promised by Jesus that encourages us in His service. Their security encourages us too. The young man turned away from Christ because he was unwilling to part with his possessions, but it is an irony of the story that he turned from possessions that were certain to possessions that were at best uncertain. Maybe he lost those possessions before the year was out. Maybe his gold was stolen. His land could have been taken. As in the prodigal's case, his friends could have grown cold and abandoned him.

This point can be made even stronger. God often allows the ungodly to amass great wealth — to their destruction. But if you are one with whom God is dealing and if you put the pursuit of riches (or anything else) before service to Christ, God may take away those riches (and other things) until you turn to Him.

Some years ago Donald Grey Barnhouse was counseling a young woman on the sidewalk in front of Tenth Presbyterian Church following an evening service. She said she was a Christian and that she wanted to follow Christ. But she wanted to be famous too. She wanted to pursue a stage career in New York. "After I have made it in the theater, I'll follow Christ completely," she said.

Barnhouse took a key out of his pocket and scratched a mark on a postal box standing on the corner. "That is what God will let you do," he said. "God will let you scratch the surface of success. He will let you get close enough to the top to know what it is, but He will never let you have it, because He will never let one of His children have anything rather than Himself."

Years later he met the girl again, and she confessed that this had indeed been her life story. She had dabbled in the stage. Once her picture had been in a national magazine. But she had never quite made it. She told Barnhouse, "I can't tell you how many times in my discouragement I have closed my eyes and seen you scratching on that postal box with your key. God let me scratch the edges, but He gave me nothing in place of Himself."

How different for those who deny themselves, take up their crosses, and follow Jesus. Their path begins with denial but ends in fulfillment, and the blessings given cannot be snatched away. Christian homes are the best and most secure of all homes. Christian friends are true, faithful friends. Even the fields and other possessions are secure in Christ's keeping and are multiplied to the extent that we use them properly in His service.

3. *Blessings blessed by God.* There is a third reason that the pro-

mise of Mark 10:29-30 encourages us to serve Christ: The blessings promised are themselves blessed by God in the sense that His favor rests on them and His power makes them supernaturally effective in assisting others.

This is evident in the blessing of the new family of God given to us as Christians. When I first preached the material appearing in the last chapter and ended by asking, "Where in this great world in which we live can there be found a place for those who imitate the Lord Jesus Christ and thus in their own persons live out the Beatitudes?" and when I responded, "There is only one place. It is the place the great of the world assigned Christ. It is the cross," some people said afterward that they were taken aback. They thought I was going to say, "It is the church. That is the one true place for those who live out the Beatitudes." That was not the point I was making then, but it is true, of course. The fellowship of those gathered around the cross *is* the fellowship of God's family, and that fellowship and the realities of that collective and renewed life are the greatest of all possible blessings for us and this world.

Where else can you find the joy that Christians have together? Where else is there peace? Where else do you find love that loves the unlovely? Where else are there consistent examples of self-sacrifice? The presence of these things is itself the greatest of all possible blessings for this world.

ENCOURAGEMENT TO TRUST

Christ's words to the disciples in Mark 10:29-30 are not just an encouragement to serve Christ, however, important as that may be. They are also an encouragement to trust Him through difficult times. We can hardly escape this point since the Lord links His promise of blessings to the phrase "and with them, persecutions," thereby indicating that although He undertakes to bless us abundantly with homes, brothers, sisters, mothers, children, and even fields, we will not enjoy these without the persecutions that inevitably come to any true follower of Christ. We will continue to have hardships until we come to possess our full inheritance in the presence of Jesus Himself in heaven.

Most persecutions come from the world. The world hates Christ, so naturally it hates those who serve Christ and live like Him. That hatred is increased when Christians are blessed by their heavenly Father.

Here the blessings of God on believers in this life are an encouragement to them to continue trusting Him in spite of the difficulties. The Christian may reason, "It is true that the world hates me; Jesus warned that this would be the case. But though the world hates me and wishes me harm, it is evident that God loves me and wishes me good. He has blessed me a hundredfold — with homes, brothers, sisters, mothers, children, and fields. Every day I see further evidence of God's favor. So I will trust Him to do me the further good of seeing me through these temptations and bringing me safe to heaven."

Other persecutions come from the devil. We must not overly emphasize this source of temptations, for the devil is a finite creature and can therefore only tempt one individual in one place at one time. He has probably never persecuted either you or anyone you know personally. Still the devil has hosts of lesser demons who work with him, and he is capable of working indirectly through mere human beings. If persecutions come from this source, God's goodness is an encouragement to trust Him through these times also.

Job is an example. Job was tempted by the devil; the Bible says so. God gave Satan permission to attack Job, first taking away his possessions, then taking away his health. The attack was so severe that Job tore his robe and shaved his head, which were traditional signs of mourning, sat in ashes, and scraped his sores, saying,

> Why did I not perish at birth,
>   and die as I came from the womb?
> Why were there knees to receive me
>   and breasts that I might be nursed? . . .
> Or why was I not hidden in the ground like
>   a stillborn child,
>   like an infant who never saw the light of day?
>   (Job 3:11-12, 16)

Job did not understand what was happening to him. Throughout the book he struggles to find out. Still he does not despair of God's goodness nor cease to trust Him. He reasons that God has blessed him in the past, that God's character is unchanged, and that He is therefore still favorably disposed toward him. He does not know why he is suffering, but he cries,

> I know that my Redeemer lives,

and that in the end he will stand upon the earth.
And after my skin has been destroyed,
   yet in my flesh I will see God;
I myself will see him
   with my own eyes — I, and not another.
                                    (Job 19:25-27)

At the end, although even then Job did not receive a full revelation of why God was allowing him to be so persecuted, Job enjoyed the renewed presence of God and was again blessed with a good home, family, and material possessions.

That is God's way with us. The afflictions of the righteous are many, but God keeps them through the afflictions. David suffered much, but he was kept by God and in the end could say, "I was young and now I am old, yet I have never seen the righteous forsaken or their children begging bread" (Psalm 37:25).

Yet I say this: The promise is for the righteous, which means for those who have been made righteous through God's grace received in following after Jesus Christ. These are great promises. They are encouragement to trust God and serve Christ. But they are for those who have not turned back to their possessions, as the rich young man did, but who rather have turned from them, forsaking everything for the surpassing joy of the excellency of knowing Jesus Christ. To these alone God promises homes, parents, children, friends, and fields — with persecutions — and in the age to come eternal life.

14

Christic with Us Always

All authority in heaven and on earth has been given to me. Therefore go and make disciples of all nations, baptizing them in the name of the Father and of the Son and of the Holy Spirit, and teaching them to obey everything I have commanded you. And surely I will be with you always, to the very end of the age.

— Matthew 28:18-20

In that great challenge to evangelism given just before His ascension, the Great Commission, Jesus commanded that His disciples disciple others. They were to lead them to faith through the preaching of the gospel, bring them into the fellowship of the church through the initiatory rite of baptism, and then, within that fellowship, continue to teach all that Jesus had commanded them. He promised that He would be with them always as they did this. What a great promise! The disciples were to live for Jesus in a hostile environment. They were to serve as His witnesses, striving to bring others to faith and help them grow in it. *But they were not to do this alone.* They were to go into all the world, but as they went they were to know that Jesus Himself would go with them.

ALL AUTHORITY

This is no weak assurance, because the One who spoke it, promising to be with His disciples, is no weak Master. Even in the days of His flesh He was powerful. Jesus opened blind eyes, healed lame persons, calmed troubled seas, and raised the dead. But in spite of this great power, in those days there were limitations — if in nothing else, Jesus was in only one place at one time. Now that has changed. Jesus is the risen Lord of glory, and this means that "*All* authority in heaven and on earth has been given to [Him]" (v. 18, my emphasis).

It is significant that Jesus used the word "authority" (NIV) and not merely the word "power," which the King James Version used to translate *exousia*. *Exousia* involves "power," but it contains the additional idea of legitimacy in the exercise of that power. A usurper might have power in the sense of mere naked power of rule (the Greek word *kratos* is used for that), but only a rightful sovereign has authority. Jesus is our rightful sovereign. He is sovereign over the whole of the created order, because He is the creator of it. It is His to begin with. The apostle John wrote, "Through him all things were made; without him nothing was made that has been made" (John 1:3). Paul wrote, "By him all things were created: things in heaven and on earth, visible and invisible, whether thrones or powers or rulers or authorities; all things were created by him and for him" (Colossians 1:16-17). Jesus also has a special authority over His own disciples in that He not only created them but redeemed them. Paul rightly declared, "You are not your own; you were bought at a price" (1 Corinthians 6:20).

Christ's declaration of His authority is the basis of the Great Commission. It has several parts.

1. *Authority in heaven.* When Jesus said that He had been given "all authority in heaven" He was making an astonishing claim. For the authority of heaven can be nothing less than God's own authority, and the claim is thus a claim to be God. Whatever Jehovah can do Jesus can do, for the authority of the Father and the authority of the Son are one authority.

Charles Spurgeon wrote,

> If it were his will to speak another world into existence, we should see tonight a fresh star adorning the brow of night. Were it his will at once to fold up creation like a worn out vesture, lo the elements would pass away, and yonder heavens would be shriveled like a scroll. The power which binds the sweet influence of the Pleiades and looses the bands of Orion is with the Nazarene; the Crucified leads forth Arcturus with his sons. Angelic bands are waiting on the wing to do the bidding of Jesus of

Nazareth, and cherubim and seraphim and the four living creatures before the throne unceasingly obey him. He who was despised and rejected of men now commands the homage of all
heaven, as "God over all, blessed for ever."[1]

It is this great Lord of glory, God over all, who has promised to
"be with [us] always, to the very end of the age."

2. *Authority over spiritual forces.* Jesus' claim to have been given
all authority in heaven probably extends also to what in other passages are described as principalities and powers, that is, all spiritual forces, including those which are demonic. Paul wrote about
these in Ephesians 6 in his classic description of the Christian's
warfare: "For our struggle is not against flesh and blood, but
against the rulers, against the authorities, against the powers of
this dark world and against the spiritual forces of evil in the heavenly realms" (v. 12). Paul was reminding the Ephesians that the
battles we wage are spiritual and the enemies we face demonic
— in our struggle to be Christ's disciples and witness for Him in
this world. But we are not to be dismayed or unnerved by this
knowledge, since these powers as well as all others have been
brought under Jesus' rightful sway. Earlier in the letter Paul wrote
that God "raised [Christ] from the dead and seated him at his right
hand in the heavenly realms, far above all rule and authority,
power and dominion, and every title that can be given, not only
in the present age but also in the one to come" (Ephesians 1:20-
21).

3. *Authority on earth.* The second part of Jesus' claim to have
been given authority concerns earth. Like the first part, it too has
several facets. The most general is what theologians call provi-
dence. It means that the events of earth (and heaven) do not unfold according to mere chance but rather are directed by God to
His own wise and perfect ends. It is a way of saying that God is in
charge. Therefore, regardless of the opposition we face, "Neither
death nor life, neither angels nor demons, neither the present nor
the future, nor any powers, neither height nor depth, nor anything else in all creation, will be able to separate us from the love
of God that is in Christ Jesus our Lord" (Romans 8:38-39).

---

1. Charles Spurgeon, "The Power of the Risen Savior" in *Metropolitan Tabernacle Pulpit*,
vol. 20 (Pasadena, Tex.: Pilgrim Publications, 1971), p. 603.

4. *Authority over His disciples.* "All authority . . . on earth" includes those who are on the earth, among them Christ's disciples. His authority obviously extends to them. It extends to their conduct, for, as we have seen, He has called them to follow Him, and this means to follow Him in obedience to His commands. He said, "You are my friends if you do what I command" (John 15:14). If we are not obeying Jesus, we are not His friends; indeed, we are not even His disciples. The authority of Christ extends to the work His disciples are called upon to do. The Great Commission emphasizes this work chiefly. It is because we are under the authority of Jesus that we are to take His gospel to the world, making "disciples of all nations, baptizing them in the name of the Father and of the Son and of the Holy Spirit, and teaching them to obey everything" He has commanded us (vv. 19-20).

The disciples of Jesus are not at liberty to determine their own type of service or set their own agenda. They are under "marching orders," as the Duke of Wellington once said, describing his own sense of being under the authority of Christ.

5. *Authority over the nations.* The fifth area to which the authority of the Lord Jesus Christ extends is those nations or people who do not yet acknowledge His authority but to whom He sends us. It is this that makes Christianity a world religion. In the ancient world there were scores of ethnic religions in which a god or gods were perceived as deities of a people but whose authorities were limited to that people only. Not so with Jesus. He was born in the ancient homeland of the Jews and spent nearly the whole of His earthly ministry among them, but His religion is not Jewish. No more is it Greek or Roman or Western European or American. It is an earth-embracing religion, because Jesus has been given authority over all the earth. His religion breaks all barriers of race, culture, language, sex, and status.

John Stott summarizes,

> The fundamental basis of all Christian missionary enterprise is the universal authority of Jesus Christ, "in heaven and on earth." If the authority of Jesus were circumscribed on earth, if he were but one of many religious teachers, one of many Jewish prophets, one of many divine incarnations, we would have no mandate to present him to the nations as the Lord and Savior of the world. If the authority of Jesus were limited in heaven, if he had not decisively overthrown the principalities and powers, we

might still proclaim him to the nations, but we would never be able to "turn them from darkness to light, and from the power of Satan unto God" (Acts 26:18).

Only because all authority on earth belongs to Christ dare we go to all nations. And only because all authority in heaven as well is his have we any hope of success.[2]

ALL NATIONS

The Great Commission contains four universals, each marked by the word all: "all authority," "all nations," "everything [or all that] I have commanded you," and "always [or all days]." The second ("all nations") refers, as I have indicated, to the universal authority of Jesus and the worldwide character of Christianity.

It is surprising that Matthew, of all the gospels, should end on this note. Each of the gospels has its unique character, as commentators have long noted. John is most universal; it presents Jesus as "the Savior of the world" (John 4:42). Luke is a Gentile or Greek book; it is usual to think of Luke's presenting Jesus to Greeks as the perfect or ideal man (as well as God incarnate). Mark seems to have been written for a Roman audience; it stresses Jesus as a miracle worker, giving less attention to His discourses than the others. By general consent Matthew is the preeminently Jewish gospel. It is written to show Jesus as the son of David and the fulfiller of the Old Testament prophecies concerning the Messiah. No other gospel is so limited to the immediate historical and ethnic climate into which Jesus was born and in which He ministered. Yet surprisingly, as I said, it is this gospel that ends on the most universal note. In the Great Commission we learn that those few Jewish disciples who had followed Jesus through the days of His ministry and who were now being commissioned formally to His service were not to limit their operations to Judaism but were rather to go to all the people and nations of the world with His gospel.

Whenever the church has done this it has been blessed and prospered. When it has not done this it has stagnated and atrophied. Why? It is because discipleship demands the Great Commission; it is an aspect of our obedience as Christ's followers, and Jesus blesses obedience. If we are following Jesus, we will go to all for whom He died.

2. John Stott, "The Great Commission" in One Race, One Gospel, One Task: World Congress on Evangelism, Berlin 1966, Official Reference Volumes, ed. Carl F. H. Henry and W. Stanley Mooneyham (Minneapolis: World Wide Publications, 1966), vol. 1, p. 46.

ALL I HAVE COMMANDED

One of the most important universals in this version of the Great Commission, particularly in our superficial age, is the command to teach those we have discipled. We are to teach them "to obey everything" Christ commanded. This is important today, because we see what seems to be the opposite. Instead of striving to teach *all* Christ commanded, many seem to be trying to eliminate as much of His teaching as possible, concentrating on an easily comprehended, unobjectionable "core" of teaching. It is a core of grace without judgment, love without justice, salvation without obedience, triumph without suffering. I am willing to concede that the motivation of some of these reductionists may be good: to win as many persons to Christ as possible. But the method is the world's, and the results (as a natural consequence) are the world's results. Disciples are not made by defective teaching. The world is not subjected to Christ's rule by demi-gospels.

Today's church needs to recapture the entire counsels of God. On the surface, where many operate, this seems the most foolish of pursuits. If we were to hold a meeting of many so-called Christians today and ask them what should be done in our time to win the entire world for Christ, it is likely that most of the discussion would center on literature campaigns, use of the media, recruitment of workers, and raising funds. Significantly, Jesus spoke of none of these things. He spoke of teaching *all* His commandments, implying that His blessing would be upon this effort as it would not fully be upon many lesser things.

I do not mean that God will not bless the proclamation of only a part of His gospel. God will bless truth however sketchily it is presented. But what I do mean is that God will only fully bless well-rounded teaching. Superficial preaching will get superficial results.

What should such teaching include? Obviously, any brief listing of doctrines is inadequate. We must teach the entire Bible. Nevertheless, faithfulness to Christ must involve at least the following.

1. *A high view of Scripture.* In our day liberal teachers are trying to undercut the church's traditionally high view of the Bible, saying that it is only a human book, that it contains errors, that it is therefore at best only relatively trustworthy or authoritative. This has produced a weak, vacillating church. It is significant that with only a few exceptions even these liberal detractors of Scripture ac-

knowledge that Jesus Himself regarded the Bible (in His case, the Old Testament) as entirely authoritative. Kirsopp Lake was no friend of historic Bible-believing Christianity, but he wrote, "The fundamentalist may be wrong; I think that he is. But it is we who have departed from the tradition, not he; and I am sorry for the fate of anyone who tries to argue with a fundamentalist on the basis of authority. The Bible and the *corpus theologicum* of the church are on the fundamentalist side."[3]

If we are to be faithful to *all* Christ's teachings, we must teach His high view of the Bible as a fundamental part of our theology.

2. *The sovereignty of God.* The English Bible translator J. B. Phillips wrote a book entitled *Your God Is Too Small.* That title, which is also a statement, might well be spoken of the great majority of professing Christians who, in their ignorance of Scripture, inevitably scale God down to their own limited and fallible perspectives. We need to capture a new, elevated sense of who God is, particularly in regard to His sovereignty. Sovereignty refers to rightful rule. So to say that God is sovereign, as the Bible does, is to say that He rules in His universe. This means that nothing is an accident, that nothing catches God off guard.

3. *The depravity of man.* Church people are willing to speak of sin in the sense that all are "less perfect than God" and need help to live godly lives. This is not offensive to anyone. But it is not the full biblical teaching. The Bible teaches that men and women are in rebellion against God (Psalm 2:1-3). It says not that they are marred by sin but that they are dead in it (Ephesians 2:1-3). It says they have been so affected by sin that even their thoughts are corrupted. "The Lord saw how great man's wickedness on the earth had become, and that every inclination of the thoughts of his heart was only evil all the time" (Genesis 6:5). So great is this depravity that a person cannot even come to Christ unless God first renews his soul and thus draws him (John 6:24).

4. *Grace.* Although it is true that in ourselves we cannot come to Christ, and so live under God's judgment, Christ teaches that God has nevertheless acted in grace toward some who were perishing. Thus, salvation is by grace alone. Jesus said, "You must be born again" (John 3:7). He declared, "All that the Father gives

3. Kirsopp Lake, *The Religion of Yesterday and Tomorrow* (Boston: Houghton, 1926), p. 61.

me will come to me" (John 6:37). He said to His Father, "I am not praying for the world, but for those you have given me, for they are yours" (John 17:9).

We cannot trace the origins of salvation farther back than by declaring that, on the basis of grace alone, God has given some of fallen humanity to Jesus for salvation. Some say, "But surely God called these because He foresaw that they would believe." But it does not say that. Others argue, "He chose them because He knew in advance that they would do something to merit salvation." But it does not say that either. What Jesus did teach is that the initiative in salvation lies entirely with God Himself and that this is found: first, in God's electing grace whereby He chooses some for salvation, entirely apart from any merit of their own (which, of course, they do not have); second, in Christ's particular work of atonement by which He bore the penalty for the sins of these people; and third, in the specific and selective work of the Holy Spirit by which He opens the blind eyes of these people to the truth of the gospel and woos their wills until they place their personal faith in Jesus as Savior.

5. *Work to do.* Although God does the great work of saving individuals, drawing them to Christ, He does not abandon them at that point but rather directs and empowers them to do meaningful work for Him. Most of Christ's teachings about discipleship fall into this area. So does Ephesians 2:10: "For we are God's workmanship, created in Christ Jesus to do good works, which God prepared in advance for us to do." It is necessary that we do these good works (as Christians in all ages have), for unless we do, we have no assurance that we are really Christ's followers. Like Jesus himself, Christians are to stand for justice and do everything in their power to comfort the sick, rescue the outcast, defend the oppressed, and save the innocent. We are also to oppose those who perpetrate or condone injustice.

6. *The security of the believer in Christ.* Jesus was strong in cautioning against presumption. He let no one think that he could presume to be a Christian while at the same time disregarding or disobeying His teachings. He said, "My sheep listen to my voice . . . and . . . follow me" (John 10:27). If we are not listening to Christ and are not following Him in faithful obedience, we are not His. However, although He cautioned against presumption, He also spoke the greatest words of assurance and confidence for those

who did follow Him. He said they would never be lost. Indeed, how could they be if God Himself is responsible for their salvation? Jesus said, "I give them eternal life, and they shall never perish; no one can snatch them out of my hand" (John 10:28).

"But," says someone, "suppose they jump out of their own accord?"

"They shall never perish," says the Lord.

"Never?"

"Never," says Jesus. "They shall never perish; no one can snatch them out of my hand."

This does not mean that there will not be dangers, of course. In fact, it implies them; for if Jesus promises that no one will succeed in snatching us from His hands, it must be because He knows that there are some who will try. The Christian will always face dangers — dangers from without, from enemies, and dangers from within. Still the promise is that those who have believed in Jesus will never be lost. The Christian may well be deprived of things. He may lose his job, his friends, his good reputation. This has happened to those who have been most faithful, particularly in times of persecution. Still, believers will not be lost. The promise is not that the ship will not go to the bottom, but that the passengers will all reach the shore. It is not that the house will not burn down, but that the people will all escape safely.

Today's Christians need to articulate these great biblical doctrines afresh, not just adopt the theology of our culture. We need to speak of the depravity of man, of man in rebellion against God, so much so that there is no hope for him apart from God's grace. We need to speak of God's electing love, showing that God enters the life of the individual in grace by His Holy Spirit to quicken understanding and draw the rebellious will to Himself. We must speak of perseverance, that God is able to keep and does keep those whom He so draws. All these doctrines and the supporting doctrines that go with them need to be proclaimed. We have to say, "This is where we stand. We do not adopt the world's theology or even the theology of the liberal church." Unless we do this we cannot consider ourselves to be faithful and obedient disciples of Jesus — or even followers at all. Without this our churches will not prosper, and our preaching and teaching will not be fully blessed.

ALWAYS

The final universal of Matthew 28:18-20 is "always" or, as the Greek literally says, "all the days, even to the consummation of the age." It is a great promise. In the first chapter of Matthew, Jesus was introduced as " 'Immanuel' — which means, 'God with us' " (Matthew 1:23). Here in the very last verse that promise is repeated and confirmed.

John Stott writes,

> This was not the first time Christ had promised them his risen presence. Earlier in this Gospel (18:20) he had undertaken to be in their midst when only two or three disciples were gathered in his name. Now, as he repeats the promise of his presence, he attaches it rather to their witness than to their worship. It is not only when we *meet* in his name, but when we *go* in his name, that he promises to be with us. The emphatic "I," who pledges his presence, is the one who has universal authority and who sends forth his people. It remains questionable, therefore, whether a stay-at-home church — disobedient to the Great Commission, and indifferent to the need of the nations — is in any position to claim or inherit the fullness of Christ's promised presence.
>
> But to those who go, who go into the world as Christ himself came into the world, who sacrifice their ease and comfort and independence, who hazard their lives in search of disciples — to them the presence of the living Christ is promised. In sending them out, he yet accompanies them. "Go," he says and, "Lo, I am with you" — with you in the person of the Holy Spirit to restrain you and direct you, to encourage and empower you. "I am with you all the days" — in days of safety and of peril, days of failure and success, days of freedom to preach and days of restriction and persecution, days of peace and of conflict and war — "I am with you all the days unto the end of the world." The promise of Christ spans the whole Gospel age. While the Christ who is speaking has only just died and been raised from death, he even now looks ahead to his return to glory. He who has just inaugurated the new age promises to be with his people from its beginning to its end, from its inauguration to its consummation, even "to the close of the age" (Matthew 28:20, RSV*).[4]

*Revised Standard Version.
4. Stott, p. 49.

It is not easy to follow Christ. He never suggested it would be. But it is far better than not following Him, for not only do we have the promise of a sure hope beyond the grave and rewards in heaven, we have the promise of the Lord's presence with us now as we seek to serve Him. His presence is to be desired above rubies. To know Him is of greater value than gold.

Other Books by James Montgomery Boice

Witness and Revelation in the Gospel of John
Philippians: An Expositional Commentary
The Sermon on the Mount
How to Live the Christian Life (originally, *How to Live It Up*)
Ordinary Men Called by God (originally, *How God Can Use Nobodies*)
The Last and Future World
The Gospel of John: An Expositional Commentary (5 volumes)
Galatians in the *Expositor's Bible Commentary*
Can You Run Away from God?
Our Sovereign God (editor)
Our Savior God: Studies on Man, Christ and the Atonement (editor)
Foundations of the Christian Faith (4-volume series):
    The Sovereign God (volume 1)
    God the Redeemer (volume 2)
    Awakening to God (volume 3)
    God and History (volume 4)
The Foundation of Biblical Authority (editor)
The Epistles of John
Does Inerrancy Matter?
Making God's Word Plain (editor)
Genesis: An Expositional Commentary (3 volumes)
The Parables of Jesus
The Minor Prophets: An Expositional Commentary (2 volumes)
The Christ of Christmas
The Christ of the Empty Tomb
Standing on the Rock

126708